A PENGUIN SPECIAL
S218
THE NEW COLD WAR
MOSCOW v. PEKIN

EDWARD CRANKSHAW

Edward Crankshaw

THE NEW COLD WAR
MOSCOW v. PEKIN

PENGUIN BOOKS

Penguin Books Ltd, Harmondsworth, Middlesex
U.S.A.: Penguin Books Inc., 3300 Clipper Mill Road, Baltimore 11, Md
AUSTRALIA: Penguin Books Pty Ltd, 762 Whitehorse Road,
Mitcham, Victoria

—

First published 1963

—

Copyright © Edward Crankshaw, 1963

CONTENTS

Chapter One

INTRODUCTORY

THIS book was started at a time when quite a strong body of opinion in the West was still refusing to take seriously the rift between the Soviet Union and the Chinese People's Republic. To uncommitted observers, whose duty or interest it was to make a close study of Communist activities, the existence of a conflict had been apparent for a number of years. But because the realities of the dispute were carefully concealed, and because in public utterances neither side attacked the other by name, it was impossible, even as late as the early autumn of 1962, to prove the extent and bitterness of the quarrel without the most elaborate documentation; and, although this had up to a point been done, very few people in the West were any the wiser because, to understand the documentation, the reader first had to master the code-language of Communist polemics. Many who should have known better were able to play down the seriousness of the rift, or to dismiss it as a 'family quarrel' (what a family!). The only conceivable reason for doing that was fear of 'wishful thinking', that hoary old inhibitor of common-sense and rational thought – though why it should appear immediately desirable, in a world striving for peace, for two of the world's greatest powers to be at each other's throats has never been clear to me.

Then, in October 1962, came the Cuban episode, and China's invasion of India. After that it was impossible for anyone to pretend that all was well between Pekin and Moscow. Soon afterwards, in December, the two sides for the first time permitted themselves to refer to each other by name. And since then the open polemics have been fast and furious.

The main purpose of this book, as originally conceived, was to demonstrate beyond all refutation the existence of the rift – seen not as a passing quarrel but as a critical breach. Once the affair became public property in December 1962 it was necessary to ask whether there was any point in finishing the book. But it did not take long to decide that it still should be written – indeed, that what was needed was a convenient outline of the genesis and development of a situation which, in one way or another, must affect the lives of all of us.

It is a situation which has come to stay. The question so frequently asked – will it come to a breach? – has long been overtaken by events. The breach is there, and, as I shall try to show in the pages that follow, it cannot be healed without a change of leadership in Pekin or Moscow, even though it may from time to time be more or less smoothly papered over. My own view is that even a change of leadership would make little difference in the long run: the causes of the conflict are bigger than men.

Since December 1962, when the existence of the dispute was for the first time formally acknowledged before all the world by both sides, we have been told in public speeches by Communist leaders and in press polemics a good deal about the opposing points of view. But these have dwelt only on the ideological aspects of the conflict: there is much more to be learnt from a close study of what was said and done in Moscow and Pekin in earlier years.

A barely concealed argument, often conducted in violent and bitter terms, has been raging since 1958. It is common knowledge today that when the Russians spoke of the Albanians and the dogmatists they meant the Chinese, that when the Chinese spoke of the Yugoslavs and the revisionists they meant the Russians. But it was not always common knowledge: indeed, for a long time a surprisingly large number of informed Western observers refused to recognize these simple equations. And even now that they are generally recognized none but the few who have been following the course of the dispute for years are much wiser.

Most people know by now that Mr Khrushchev has accused the Chinese of being too reckless in their talk of inevitable war, of encouraging and supporting revolutionary struggles which might lead to war, of endangering the unity of the Communist world by refusing to abide by majority decisions taken by the fraternal parties in conclave. But for the thousands whose imaginations were caught by Mao Tse-tung's characterization of the 'imperialists' as 'paper tigers', and Khrushchev's retort that these paper tigers have 'nuclear teeth', very few realize that when Khrushchev attacks the Chinese for their warlike policies he is trailing a red herring. It is true enough that the Chinese leaders do not appear to have grasped the full implications of nuclear warfare (until a very few years ago the same was true of Western leaders, to say nothing of the Russians). It is true that they have boasted that if 300 million Chinese were killed there would still be 300 million left to enjoy the triumph of Communism. It is true that like many Americans and some British, but unlike Khrushchev, they feel that in the last resort it is nothing but cowardly defeatism to quail before the nuclear threat. But it is not true to suggest that they would welcome a nuclear war. Khrushchev knows this very well; but he contrives in his letters and speeches to suggest the contrary – for the simple reason that by playing on the fear of nuclear annihilation among the fraternal parties he has been able to frighten them into supporting him against China, and, at the same time, obscure certain of the basic issues, which have nothing at all to do with Communism and are only indirectly concerned with war and peace.

As far as the outside world is concerned, the real depth of the conflict, its range and bitterness, has been obscured by the language in which it has been conducted. Apart from occasional twinkles of very un-Marxist Chinese imagery (which irritate Khrushchev exceedingly: will the Chinese comrades, he was to say at the Moscow Conference in 1960, be good enough to refrain from using Chinese phrases – 'paper tigers' for American Presidents, 'let a hundred flowers bloom' for relaxation of central control – and try to express themselves more decorously in proper Marxist terms which everyone could understand?) – apart from these, the charges flung about by both sides are formulated in conventional Leninist jargon of the usual dreary kind. It is a jargon in which 'revisionism' means betrayal of the ideals of the revolution, in which 'dogmatism' means criminal obscurantism, in which 'fractionalism' is mortal sin. Thus, when a solemn debate is presented under the head 'How should the present epoch be defined in Marxist terms?' the intelligent reader, untrained in Communist linguistics, may be forgiven for passing by on the other side: he does not really care and he thinks it has nothing to do with him. This is erroneous; for under this academic and esoteric head issues are being debated, not coolly but with passion, which will affect the whole future of the Communist movement, and therefore our own lives.

What has been at issue here, fundamentally, is whether there is to be any future for a unified Communist movement; whether there will be two Communist popes, one in Moscow, one in Pekin. How would a schism of this kind affect the rest of the Communist world? Are we out of date in continuing to arm ourselves against what we take to be a dynamic and monolithic force inspired by an untouchable ideology? Should we stop thinking in terms of the Communist menace and more about balances of power?

Behind the mystification of the Communist code-language there lies a deeper level of uncertainty. To what extent are we to take the ideological quarrel at its face value, as a dispute among Communists? To what extent is this ideological wrangle a disguise, assumed to mislead the fraternal parties as well as the outside world, for old-fashioned nationalism and neo-imperialism?

Before we can begin to contemplate these fundamental issues we must discover as exactly as possible what the position is as between Moscow, Pekin, and the other main centres of Communist authority, today. This means first that we have to glance at the historical background of the existing rift and then examine the formation of the rift itself, which is of an extreme complexity. We shall see that the quarrel, as it develops, is conducted in almost exclusively ideological terms; but it will soon be apparent that issues other than purely ideological disputes are at stake. At this stage there is no need to comment further along these lines, which will emerge of their own accord as the narrative progresses. To begin with it is enough to remember that the Soviet Union is a great European power, that China is a great Asian power with a proud and antique past. It is worth bearing in mind one or two other great question-marks of history. Perhaps one will do. Was the bloody conflict between Rome and the Counts of Toulouse in the thirteenth century an ideological conflict? Was it purely, or even primarily, an affair of heresy-hunting? Or was the destruction of the Cathars no more than an incident in the process of the unification of France, with the popes supporting the new French dynasty as a counterpoise to what was left of imperial power? There is no need to push analogies of this kind: dubious as they are, they are starting points rather than solutions. For the time being we must take the issues in dispute at their face value. But before even this can be done it will be necessary to glance at the genesis of the Chinese revolution in so far as this was influenced by Soviet policy. It is possible to summarize fairly briefly the ostensible issues at stake, but it is impossible to arrive at an adequate understanding of those issues without some background knowledge of the general conditions of the Soviet Union and China when, in 1957, those issues, hitherto dormant, began to shape themselves. It will then be found that besides being an enthralling drama in its own right, the tale, as it unfolds, will illuminate most usefully the whole area of Communist thought and intention, so often obscured not only by Leninist jargon but also, and less excusably from our point of view, by the refusal of Western politicians and commentators to examine the development of Communist power in the light of the history of human institutions – or even in the light of human behaviour as commonly displayed in our everyday lives.

It is necessary to say a word about sources, and I do this here in the body of the book, instead of in a separate note, because the narrative cannot exist apart from its sources, and these are various and tricky in the extreme.

Not for the student of Soviet or Chinese affairs the revealing press conference, the inspired partisan leak, the questions and answers in the House of Commons or the Congressional Committee, the off-the-record confidences of responsible politicians, the revealing polemics of party warfare, the findings of more or less detached commissions of inquiry, the sudden flare-up of a national scandal, the prime minister or the president defensively extracting himself under vicious pressure from indefensible situations, the mass of reliable (if often heavily slanted) government statistics about every aspect of social and economic life, the indiscretions of technical journals, and all the rest of the paraphernalia of quasi-democratic society. On the other hand, and especially since the death of Stalin in 1953, there has been a great deal more information in the Soviet press and in the public speeches of the Soviet leaders than at first sight appears. Of course the press is rigidly controlled. Of course nothing can be mentioned or discussed unless the government so desires. Of course there is no criticism of the higher leadership. To take only one example of the thoroughness of government control, and that one the most relevant to our purpose: the first serious development in the Sino–Soviet conflict occurred in 1958. By 1959 the Chinese were attacking hard in their own press, without ever mentioning the Soviet Union by name, and Khrushchev began to counter-attack. In the summer and early winter of 1960 there took place the two critical meetings, at Bucarest and Moscow, in which Khrushchev personally confronted the Chinese and exchanged insults with them – at Moscow in the presence of delegates from eighty-one Communist Parties. No reference was made in the Communist press anywhere in the world to the content of either of these two meetings; and thereafter the quasi-public debate continued to be pursued in veiled terms. It was not until the 22nd Party Congress in Moscow in October 1961 that Khrushchev, still not referring directly to the Chinese, delivered his onslaught on the Albanians, by whom he clearly meant the Chinese. The quarrel continued to rage, with the Chinese saying Tito when they meant Khrushchev and the Russians saying Enver Hoxha when they meant Mao Tse-tung – until, at the round of European Communist Party Congresses in the winter of 1962–3, China was at last attacked publicly and by name in Rome, Prague, East Berlin, and elsewhere.

Thus for five years the quarrel had been in progress without a single direct reference to it occurring in either the Chinese or the Soviet press. But (and this is the important point) both Khrushchev and Mao Tse-tung had, all this time, been desirous of informing the leaders of all fraternal parties of the state of the conflict and the issues at stake; further, of advancing their respective causes. Hence the sustained double-talk polemics.

This would have been enough in itself to indicate to the devoted student of Communist affairs, accustomed to reading between the lines (just as the Communists themselves are required to read between the lines), the general outline of the ideological aspects of the conflict with some exactitude. But something more was required to bring home the bitterness and the passion of the conflict and also the inter-State acerbities as between the Soviet Union and the Chinese People's Republic. This was supplied early in 1961 when, by one of those strokes of fortune so rarely vouchsafed earnest workers in this stony field, I myself was able to publish in the *Observer* the inside story of what had taken place at the Bucarest and Moscow conferences of the previous year. For some time the material upon which this account was based (referred to in the Notes, page 165) was regarded as suspect by many and denounced as a forgery by some. Thanks, however, to the eagerness of the leaders of a number of European Communist Parties – especially the Italian, the French, and the Belgian – to justify to their followers their support of Khrushchev at the critical Moscow Conference of November 1960, by the end of 1962 enough had been published in the Party literature of these countries to confirm up to the hilt what I had written in February 1961 and, indeed, to add to it. Even more importantly, in no particular at all have the details presented in those *Observer* articles ever been contradicted.

By the time this book is published a new chapter in the continuing story will have opened. In the spring of 1963 Moscow and Pekin both sought to escape the dead-lock by engaging in the most intricate manoeuvring for position, each seeking to convince the fraternal parties of its rectitude, each trying to saddle the other with the blame for persistent discord. The Chinese invited Khrushchev to Pekin, the Russians invited Mao to Moscow – each knowing that the other must refuse. In the end it was agreed that the Chinese should send a special delegation to Moscow in July to thresh things out with the Russians. But even if this meeting manages to achieve some sort of a formal reconciliation, the basic differences will remain. The following pages will indicate why this must be so.

11 June 1963

Chapter Two

THE ARRIVAL OF RED CHINA

I

THE Communist bloc consists of all those countries living under Communist governments which, until a very short time ago, recognized the Soviet Union as their mainstay and preceptor. It consists of the Soviet Union itself, the 'People's Democracies' of Eastern and Central Europe (but not Yugoslavia), the Chinese People's Republic, North Korea, North Vietnam, Outer Mongolia, and Cuba. It embraces the lives of over a billion souls, rather more than a third of the total population of the globe.

But it is by no means as solid and homogeneous an entity as it is made out to be, by the West as well as by the Communists, and the strains and stresses within it are not only of absorbing interest in themselves: they also bear very sharply and heavily on the future of us all.

These strains and stresses, or (to borrow a term from the Communists) internal contradictions, arise naturally from the historical and national backgrounds of the various members of the bloc, from differences in their pre-revolutionary social and economic development, from the elementary facts of geography, and from conflicting ambitions. The most striking and important of these contradictions arises from the conflict between Moscow and Pekin, which has only recently been officially, or publicly, recognized for what it is. But there are others. And in tracing and analysing the course of the Sino–Soviet conflict it will be necessary to elucidate less spectacular but no less important contradictions within the Communist bloc as a whole.

The non-Communist world is acutely, sometimes paralysingly, aware of its own weaknesses, its own internal contradictions. If only to see these in an improved perspective, so that they may be faced with calm and resolution and imagination, it would be well advised to cease thinking always in terms of its own vulnerability and take an interested look at the fearful problems only partly concealed by what is left of Stalin's iron curtain.

The heart of the Communist bloc, in every sense of the word, is the Soviet Union itself. This vast and still largely unknown land has been run for getting on for half a century by self-styled Communists – that is to say, by men deriving their authority from Marx and Lenin. They are committed to a political theory which they are not content to offer as one theory among others. Indeed, the theory itself calls for the necessary elimination of all other theories and all systems of government other than the Soviet system – thus for the ultimate unification of all the peoples in the world in a vast Communist international.

Its 220 million people, comprehending many races, but dominated absolutely by Russians, have been driven to achieve, through misery, privation, and sacrificial toil, dominated for decades by police terror, a formidable military power and an economic base which, in certain important aspects, can rival the most advanced material achievements of the West. After the war, under a tyrant of genius, it was able to use this power to impose its own system of government on a great part of eastern and central Europe, including a number of countries where the standard of living had previously been very much higher than that of the Soviet Union itself. It sought to penetrate still deeper into Europe, while at the same time inciting colonial peoples in Asia and Africa and oppressed peoples in Latin America to rise up against their European masters and their reactionary governments, too often sustained by Western commercial and strategic interests. The outcome was a head-on collision between the embattled might of the Soviet Union and the United States, each striving by all means short of total war to throw the other.

Into this arena, on 1 October 1949, burst the new People's Government of China, headed by a group of men, inspired by Marxist-Leninist ideas, who, for twenty years, had been fighting – fighting first for their lives, then for territory, then for final dominion. They expelled from the Chinese mainland the Kuomintang Government, presided over by Marshal Chiang Kai-shek, who was not only America's darling but also, paradoxically, a protégé of Moscow. These philosopher warriors

owed their way of thought, their discipline, and their strategy
to the Moscow Communists, and were eager to repay this debt.
But there was little more that they owed to Moscow. Like
Marshal Tito, but on a far grander scale, Mao Tse-tung owed
his victory to his own strength, ruthlessness, and resolution, and
to nothing else at all.

Tito had achieved his Communist revolution through the
rigours, the privations, and the atrocities of war, partisan war
and civil war, helped not at all by Stalin; helped rather by the
Western allies, while Stalin discouraged his impetuosity lest he
should disturb Soviet power relations with America and Britain.
Yet all the time he had been sustained by the Soviet example and
regarded Stalin as his venerated master.

Mao Tse-tung had followed the same course. But whereas
Tito had spent his apprenticeship moving about Europe in disguise, conspiring and intriguing, now agitating in the underground, now acting as a courier for Stalin, Mao Tse-tung had
fought his way across the length and breadth of China.

As far as Stalin was concerned, the Chinese comrades were
expendable. During the Second World War, he had been prepared to sacrifice the Yugoslav Communists to the interests of
the Soviet Union as a power. Before the war he had treated the
German Communists in the same way. Even earlier he had done
the same with the Chinese. In the late 1920s Stalin had been far
less interested in forwarding the Leninist revolution in China
than in building up some sort of stable Chinese regime as a
useful ally in face of the threat from Japan, or Japan allied with
Germany or Britain. So he had told Mao Tse-tung to suspend
the revolutionary struggle and cooperate with the Kuomintang.
The result was that the Kuomintang gained in strength and
confidence and soon, in the person of Chiang Kai-shek – in 1927
one young General among others – turned on the Communists,
killed many, and caused the rest to scatter.

Mao Tse-tung took to the hills with the remnants of a shattered Communist Party. These he built up in face of appalling
difficulty until he was ready to face that epic journey which was
to become known as the Long March. Like Moses, he led his
people into the wilderness with nothing to sustain them but a
vision of the promised land. The march from the south to the

north, where, in Yennan, Mao Tse-tung was able to make contact with Soviet Communists, the famous Long March, lasted almost exactly a year. It was less of a march than a running fight, marked by a number of pitched battles as well as innumerable skirmishes with the forces of the local war-lords and of the Kuomintang. One hundred thousand set out on that march, which straggled over 5,000 miles. Half the original body were dead by the time Yennan was reached, but the survivors were augmented all the time by new recruits. Everywhere the Communists established themselves for a few days, or weeks, they set up local Soviets to organize and govern the country on Russian lines. When they passed on, the peasants immediately relapsed into their old ways; but, all the same, over a vast area of China there were now men who had had experience and training, however fleeting, in the techniques of Communist organization and rule.

This epic migration, which was to become a legend, with all the suffering it involved, may not have been necessary. For, ironically, after quarrelling bitterly with Chiang Kai-shek, Stalin in 1936, the year after the Long March, decided to make it up with him in face of the renewed Japanese menace. Once more Mao Tse-tung was told to cooperate with the man who had been his scourge. Once more Chiang Kai-shek was recognized by Stalin as a formal ally in face of the Japanese. And this state of affairs persisted until the defeat of Japan in 1945. Stalin was too late to play an effective part in this defeat (which, nevertheless, would not have been possible without Russia's colossal and decisive effort against Germany in the West), but not too late to take the credit for it, or to occupy a great part of Manchuria, the industrial heart of China torn from her by the Japanese. The Soviet Union set about the systematic looting of Manchuria, behaving as though she saw no prospect of Communist victory in China. But this time Mao Tse-tung was keeping his own counsel. In the teeth of Stalin's advice he determined to wage a war to the end against the Kuomintang, and this he did. On 20 April 1949 the Chinese Communist forces crossed the Yangtse and the end was in sight. During the summer of 1949 Stalin recognized what was happening, and although he still maintained diplomatic relations with the Kuomintang, as the legitimate government of China, he re-opened Soviet consulates on Communist-held territory. On 30 September the Chinese People's Republic was formally inaugurated, and, next day, Mao Tse-tung announced that the People's Government was the only legal government in China.

A few days later the Soviet press resounded with exultant tributes to the power and glory of the great Chinese revolutionary movement, the triumph of which had sounded the death-knell of Western imperialism in Asia and the tocsin for the toilers of the East in their innumerable millions. Chiang Kai-shek was driven into the sea and across it to Taiwan, or the island of Formosa. The Communist bloc was augmented overnight by the adherence of the most populous, the most enduring, perhaps the most industrious, nation in the world.

3

In the previous year, with the defection of Yugoslavia, it had suffered a heavy loss. Marshal Tito had quarrelled with Stalin, who then pronounced anathema upon him, had him expelled from the Cominform, and expected him to die of fright. He had quarrelled because the Yugoslav revolution had been his own revolution, a national affair, owing nothing to direct Soviet aid. He was not going to have the Russians ordering Yugoslavia about as they ordered about the Poles, the East Germans, the Hungarians, the Rumanians, the Bulgarians, and, lastly, the Czechs. The Communist governments of all these countries were headed then by men who were nothing but Stalin's puppets, front-men for the real power, which consisted of Soviet guns and tanks. In all these countries the majority of the population were anti-Communist (as indeed they still were in the Soviet Union itself). Without Soviet power behind them the local Communists would not have had a chance. The majority in Yugoslavia too were anti-Communist; but at least the Yugoslav Communists, under Tito, had won power by their own fighting worth and terrifying discipline – as the Russian Bolsheviks had done before them, as the Chinese Communists were to do after them. Stalin was out-raged when he discovered that the Yugoslav Communists were prepared to answer him back, were not prepared to hand over their own newly-won prize to Soviet overlords who tried to operate with the same disregard for national feelings that they showed in Poland or Hungary.

Thus the situation in the Communist world in October 1949 was as follows: the Soviet Union, run by men who had seized power for themselves, unaided, in 1917, was absolute master of a large part of central and eastern Europe, which it ruled through what can only be called Quislings, bitterly resented by majorities which varied from land to land, who saw their living standards being painfully reduced towards the Soviet level and their cherished freedoms, their religions even, smashed by alien might. It had quarrelled with Yugoslavia, which had refused to submit to this treatment. It now had to welcome into the fold a vast new country, three times more numerous than itself, and led by men who had achieved their revolution the hard way, on their own merits, as Tito had achieved his. The Soviet Union, moreover, had penetrated deeply into the China which from now on must be its greatest ally; and, by looting Manchuria, had severely weakened the country's industrial potential. There were a number of unresolved questions which could only be settled to Moscow's disadvantage if the great new Communist state was to retain its self-respect: the position of Inner Mongolia and Sinkiang, the matter of the Russian-operated Chinese Eastern Railway, the future of Dairen and Port Arthur. All these, unless they were to make for standing conflict between Moscow and Pekin, had to be sorted out.

Chapter Three

SEEDS OF CONFLICT

I

FROM October 1949 until the death of Stalin in 1953 relations between Moscow and Pekin were frequently uneasy but never, as far as is known, really difficult. Outstanding questions were settled; trade pacts were signed. Both Stalin and Mao were above all concerned first with economic recovery from the devastation of war, then with securing their own gains. Stalin had to rebuild a largely shattered industry and agriculture, while consolidating his new empire in eastern and central Europe. Mao had to establish and elaborate his central government throughout the length and breadth of China, to build up industry with what Russian help he could get, and to defend himself against possible American aggression. We do not know what miscalculations in Moscow and Pekin led to the Korean war in June 1951; but we do know that Stalin, while giving some help to North Korea, kept out of that war, and that Mao followed suit until the crossing of the 38th parallel by General MacArthur's troops appeared to threaten China with invasion.

The most interesting aspect of this period was a certain mutual reserve between Stalin and Mao about each other's ideological pretensions. Although the Soviet press hailed the Chinese revolution as a world-shattering event, as the beginning of a forest-fire which would quickly spread through Asia and beyond, China was not at first treated as part of the Communist international. She did not become a member of the Cominform. It was made clear in the Soviet Party journals that she had a long passage to work before she could regard herself as a Socialist country. Above all the Russians went out of their way to emphasize that there was no question of regarding Pekin as a headquarters for the organization of Asian Communism.

The Chinese, on their side, at first laid a good deal of emphasis on their own special way, as a blue-print for colonial and ex-colonial countries everywhere. Echoing and developing the thesis expressed by Liu Shao-ch'i in a famous interview with Anna Louise Strong in 1946, they claimed in their propaganda that Mao was an independent prophet and theorist and that his writings embodied a new and independent ideology: the path marked out by them for other undeveloped countries was referred to as 'Mao's Road'. The Russians would have none of this, spoke and wrote always as though Mao was bound by Stalin's theories, and ignored all Chinese claims to ideological autonomy.

Naturally they were well aware of these claims. This was the time when Stalin's 'personality cult' was at its zenith. He was the sun of the Communist world, the great leader and teacher, the all-wise, all-knowing. It is absurd to imagine that he and those close to him can have viewed Mao's pretensions to a mind of his own with anything but profound misgiving, not to say anger. But in the time of Stalin differences inside the bloc were not allowed to show. What happened when this prohibition was broken was displayed by Stalin's violent and brutal reaction to Marshal Tito's criticisms of the Soviet comrades. Erroneously, Stalin imagined that he could soon make an end of Tito and substitute a puppet leader of the Yugoslav Communists. But he knew very well that he could not treat Mao in this way. All he could do was apply, behind the scenes, a certain economic pressure. And this, it is clear enough, he did. When in February 1950 a Chinese delegation travelled to Moscow to negotiate a new trade and communications agreement, the negotiations dragged on until mid-June, ten days before the outbreak of the Korean War. After that much less was heard about Mao Tse-tung as a prophet and an Asian Karl Marx.

These early points of friction, revealing themselves so soon after the triumph of the Chinese revolution, which Stalin had discouraged, are important to remember. There is a tendency in the West to assume that the conflict between the great Communist powers has arisen almost entirely because of ideological differences between Khrushchev and Mao, with Khrushchev seen as the exponent of the 'soft' line, Mao of the 'hard'. Khrushchev himself, for his own reasons, has done his best to reinforce this assumption, which is, however, unfounded. The basic difference, which underlies all others, arises from the

Chinese rejection of the pretensions of Moscow as the Communist Rome and the corollary of this, the subservience of a great Asian power to a great European power. This difference was latent while Stalin was alive, and there is no reason to suppose that had he lived another ten years it would not have come to the surface. It was suppressed rigidly for some years after 1950, because China depended absolutely on her alliance with Russia, both for help with her economy and for backing vis-à-vis America – and because, after Stalin's death in 1953, the first imperative was to maintain an appearance of monolithic unity.

It is true that as the conflict developed the opposition of 'hard' and 'soft' became increasingly important, and it could be argued that, given the comparative state of development of the Soviet Union and Communist China, it was inevitable. But the opposition between the two powers went deeper than this. And, indeed, there is reason to suppose that Mao originally backed Khrushchev against Malenkov because he approved of the way in which Khrushchev's mind was working and also because he believed that with Khrushchev in command China would find it more easy to influence the Soviet Union.

Certainly in the years immediately after Stalin's death Chinese policy towards the outer world, apart from the imperialist powers, was more experimental than Soviet policy, was indeed very close to the policy Khrushchev himself was later to expound.

At the Bandung Conference in 1955 the Chinese proclaimed solidarity with the neutralist governments in face of imperialism and laid down five principles of international affairs – the recognition of national independence, national sovereignty, equality between nations, non-interference in internal affairs, and self-determination – which were in advance of Soviet thought and were only endorsed later by the Russians. Again, in 1957 Mao's short-lived experiment of the 'hundred flowers' was markedly in advance of Khrushchev's experimentation in the first period of the 'thaw'. In a word, from 1955 until the great 'leftward' swing towards the end of 1957, Mao himself was actively pursuing certain policies which were later, as practised by Khrushchev, to become anathema. The situation, thus, is not without its paradoxes. What went wrong?

It is impossible to say with certainty the precise date at which the Chinese decided that they had to challenge Khrushchev. Later on we shall see, when we come to consider the climacteric year, 1960, that Khrushchev gave 1959 as the beginning of the conflict, accusing China of then beginning to violate the Moscow Declaration of November 1957, a policy document signed by all the bloc parties after their meeting to celebrate the fortieth anniversary of the Russian revolution. But the Chinese themselves gave 1956 as the critical year, the year of the 20th Party Congress at which Khrushchev made his secret speech denouncing Stalin. In their latest polemics the Chinese go back much farther; but, looking back, it seems that 1958 was the crucial year. It was then that Mao decided that Khrushchev himself, whom, until then, he had backed in his struggle for power, was not a fit person to stand alone at the head of a world Communist movement which included China.

2

The most spectacular aspect of the 20th Party Congress, the denunciation of Stalin and the 'personality cult', is now so familiar that nothing need be said about it here. The process was started in open session by Mikoyan, who questioned in a way until then unprecedented and undreamed of Stalin's claims to the mantle of Lenin. It was concluded when, in secret session, Khrushchev accused his late master not only of fearful mistakes but also of untold crimes. Even so, it was not a blanket denunciation. Khrushchev was careful to speak only of Stalin's crimes against the Party, and even here he was selective. He had little or nothing to say about Stalin's crimes against the Soviet people – the crimes, for example, committed during the collectivization – or against the peoples of eastern and central Europe. He said enough, however, to establish Stalin as a monster in the eyes of all who heard him speak, and his speech was clearly precipitated by the struggle for power within the Kremlin: Khrushchev took a gamble, presenting himself as the man who was ready to lead the country out of dark places, while others dragged their feet.

But something else happened at that Congress, even more important in the long run than the attack on Stalin, though quite overshadowed by this at the time. Khrushchev in his public address – his formal report to the Congress on the opening day – proclaimed two radical amendments to the Leninist canon. These amendments were to change the whole face of Communism, and they stand at the heart of the Sino–Russian conflict, justifying up to the hilt the charges of 'revisionism' later to be levelled by the Chinese against the Soviet party in general and Khrushchev in particular. They concerned the inevitability of war and the necessity of violent revolution on the march towards global Communism. It is impossible to make head or tail of the conflict, as it developed, unless their significance is understood.

Lenin's belief in the inevitability of war, so long as capitalism existed anywhere on the surface of the globe, was absolute and fundamental. Wars, he thought, arose from economic causes inherent in the capitalist system. Under economic pressure, or driven by material greed, capitalist societies must be driven with fatal inevitability to fight each other for markets. And, moreover, this was a good thing. It was a good thing because war is the breeding ground of revolution. Anything which put an intolerable strain on capitalist societies and dislocated their economies must be good for Communism. To this extraordinary creature it did not matter that millions of the ordinary working men and women would also suffer and die as a result of war: one can't make an omelette without breaking eggs, he would say. Presumably, therefore, the more broken eggs the bigger the omelette; certainly, the more the masses suffered now, the sooner their survivors and heirs would enter into their inheritance. So he formulated his doctrine that the way to world revolution must lie through a series of bloody conflicts.

It was the same with the revolutions themselves, as they took place in individual countries: the more violent the better. For Lenin, dedicated to the fulfilment of 'scientific' Marxism (dedicated also, let us not forget, to ideals of social justice and equity), the most detested creature was the social reformer, the non-Marxist radical. His hatred for the capitalist bosses was quite different in kind from his hatred of liberals and agrarian reformers and social democrats outside the Bolshevik fold. The capitalists could not help themselves. They had their part to play in the unfolding of the great dialectic. It was their historical

role to rise and then be overthrown. They could not be blamed
for being capitalists any more than a tiger can be blamed for
eating flesh. Without the capitalist, Marxism could not have
been. Had there been no capitalism it would have been necessary
to invent it.

But social reformers of all kinds were anathema. They had no
place in the great design. They were, at best, the perverse
lackeys of capitalism, and for the simple reason that every
amelioration of the condition of the workers, the proletariat –
every wage increase, every curtailment of working hours, every
step forward in the direction of social security, every increase in
insurance benefits, every rise of whatever kind in the standard of
living – could only make the workers more satisfied with their
lot and postpone the day when they would rise in violence against
their employers and sweep them and their system away.

In a word Lenin and his Bolsheviks – but Lenin had to use
the lash to keep many of his followers up to scratch – starting
with the noble ideal of social justice and inspired by compassion
for the oppressed and indignation against the oppressor, fell so
in love with a particular system calculated to realize these ideals,
the Marxist system as interpreted by them, that at some point the
means, the Marxist revolution, became in their eyes more
important than the end, social justice; and any attempt to achieve
the end by other means was seen as a vicious heresy. Revolutions
had to be achieved through violence. Social reform, as such, was
wicked: it meant compromising with the enemy. This is why,
for example, Soviet Communists have for so long spoken with
more hatred of the Gaitskells and the Bevans (all one to them)
than of the Macmillans and the Institute of Directors. On a
different level, but by a simple extension of the argument to the
international sphere, this is why Stalin regarded Mr Nehru as a
more dangerous enemy than Mr Dulles. Dulles was a straightforward product of capitalism, with his appointed role to play.
Nehru was neither fish nor fowl: he was a bad red herring. If
this kind of attitude seems perverse to the point of insanity, it
should be remembered that it has illustrious precedents: for one,
Rome has always pursued the Christian heretic with more
righteous wrath and bitterness than the non-Christian.

These two doctrines of Lenin, with a number of corollaries – the doctrine of the inevitability of war and of the need for violent revolution – were written into the sacred books of Communism and remained a fundamental part of the canon long after they had clearly been overtaken by events. The main event that overtook them, perceptible, one would have said, even to a Leninist, was the perfection of the atom bomb. When Lenin was dreaming his dreams of the capitalist powers embroiling each other, and perhaps Russia too, in 'bloody conflicts' which would dislocate their economies and drive the common people in despair to revolt against their masters, wars were strictly limited affairs. After a few Passchendaeles, a few Verduns, the killing off of ten or twenty million souls, they came to an end, and life went on as before, except that in this country or that the old governments would have fallen and been replaced by revolutionary committees. An individual of Lenin's calibre could view the casualties of the First World War, even of the Second, with equanimity: for a man who was kind to children and sorry for the underdog he had a remarkable capacity for seeing only the broad movements of history. But the advent of nuclear weapons changed all that. The impact of machine-gun bullets and high explosive, even gas, on the human flesh could be seen as a liberating influence: those who survived would say 'No more war' and embrace the true faith. But who was going to survive a nuclear war? And what was the good of a war that might well annihilate, or reduce to an atomic desert, the holy land of the revolution itself?

In fairness to Stalin, it should be recorded that a few months before his death, in October 1952 that is, he began to show signs of grappling with this problem: for the 19th Party Congress he produced a radical gloss on the Lenin doctrine. In a long and not strikingly original paper called 'Problems of Economics', he allowed himself to hazard the view that although so long as capitalism existed wars could not be avoided it might now be possible (the 'Socialist camp' having become so strong) for the Soviet Union to keep out of them, leaving the capitalist powers to tear themselves to pieces in the struggle for markets.

This was by no means the complete answer; but it was a step in the direction of reality. It was not developed as no doubt Stalin intended to develop it because, soon afterwards, he found himself involved in preparations for a new domestic purge of his most trusted colleagues, presented in the *grand guignol* setting of the notorious 'doctor's plot'. Then, almost immediately, he himself most providentially died.

In the confusion following Stalin's death there was no time for ideological re-thinking. Malenkov, as Prime Minister, did go so far as to say that a nuclear war might destroy Communism as well as capitalism; but Khrushchev, as First Secretary of the Communist Party, denied this hotly. The Communist countries, he conceded, would suffer severe damage; but they could not be destroyed: only capitalism would be destroyed, and Communism would survive. Thus, between 1953 and 1955, the atom bomb, and Russia's attitude to nuclear war, was reduced to a gambit in a personal struggle for power.

Until, in February 1956, Khrushchev did the logical thing and came out flatly with the statement that times had changed, that the 'Socialist camp' was now so strong that nobody dared attack it (the peace-loving masses in the 'imperialist camp' would not allow their masters to try), that, therefore, war must no longer be regarded as 'fatally inevitable'. Furthermore, times having changed, and the peace-loving masses, inspired and sustained by the Soviet Union, having grown so strong, it was more than conceivable that in 'certain countries' Communism would be achieved not through violent revolution but by natural evolution through, perhaps, parliamentary means.

The world should have heaved a profound sigh of relief: Moscow was moving into the atomic age. It did not, first because it was completely taken up with Khrushchev's revelations about Stalin; secondly because it regarded his words about war and revolution as the usual Communist doubletalk, not understanding the solemnity of the occasion: Communists, not even Khrushchev, do not take the word of Lenin in vain. Only the most stringent pressure of reality could have pushed Khrushchev, or any other Communist leader, into the solemn proclamation that a central point of Leninist doctrine had been outmoded and must be radically revised.

But the Communists themselves understood. Sophisticated Party leaders in Europe and elsewhere, who had been crippled for years in their appeal to the masses by this ball and chain of the inevitability of war and violent revolution, rejoiced in their new freedom. Others, with their eyes on vast areas inhabited by still primitive societies, still thinking in terms of war and violence, should have been disturbed, above all the Chinese. Were the Russians preparing to abandon the revolutionary struggle simply because they were afraid of a few hydrogen bombs? (This was later to be the Chinese line. But Pekin made no protest at the time. In the light of its subsequent stand this seems strange.) The logic of the situation was clear even in 1956. Nuclear war could cripple, or destroy, the Soviet Union: therefore it was foolish to go on saying that war was inevitable. The fostering of revolution through violence might lead to local war, which could all too easily develop into a major nuclear war: therefore in all such cases Communism must be achieved by means other than violent revolution. If violent revolution was, in certain cases, to be abjured, the heart was removed from Marxism, from Leninism. Communists would be reduced to working indefinitely for social reform, for the amelioration of the conditions of the masses. What, in the last resort, would remain to differentiate them from despicable reformists?

Chapter Four

THE KHRUSHCHEV LINE

I

THIS was the basic, profoundly troubling question which was to underlie subsequent developments, moulding them, until, in the winter of 1962–3, it broke surface. At first it was perhaps imperfectly apprehended, certainly imperfectly formulated. There was no question in 1956 of the Chinese accusing Khrushchev of betraying Marxist-Leninism, of betraying the revolution. It is to be doubted whether they knew what Khrushchev was doing any more than he knew himself. On his part there was no conscious act of betrayal. On the contrary, in 1956, there can be no doubt at all, he saw himself as the man who was saving the spirit of Leninism from the corruption of Stalinism. Admittedly he was undertaking to modify Lenin's doctrines about war and violent revolution. But he could say, as he did, that Lenin's teachings were not to be regarded as a set of sacred texts, each valid in all circumstances for all time, but, rather, as a coherent body of doctrine to serve as a guiding light in a world which was constantly changing, technologically, socially, politically; and much of this bewildering change was the direct result of practical application of this doctrine, first in Russia, then elsewhere. Nobody, not even the greatest prophet, not even Lenin, could have foreseen the hydrogen bomb; therefore it was the proper task of good Leninists to adapt his teachings to this new fact. Self-styled Leninists who failed to respond in this manner could only be stigmatized as dogmatists, clinging to the letter of Lenin's teaching and neglecting its spirit, parroting texts which they did not try to understand.

But at the time of the 20th Party Congress, in 1956, Khrushchev was in fact in the process of revising Lenin's teaching far more radically than he realized. 'Life itself', to use his own favourite tag, was carrying him along and sweeping him into a new position which he himself, intent on riding the wave, did not then at all clearly appreciate. The Chinese failed also to appreciate it, but for a different reason: their vision of the outside world, including the Soviet Union, was so limited and distorted that they were quite unable to perceive the true nature of the forces, both inside and outside Russia, to which Khrushchev was half-consciously, half-unconsciously adjusting himself. This meant that in 1956 it was quite impossible for them to see the direction in which he was moving. It was only later, when this direction became all too clear, that they started to register a protest. Then, looking back, they could truthfully say that the trouble began with the 20th Party Congress; but, without admitting a gross failure of prescience, they could not admit that they had failed to see just what was happening at the time.

2

What was happening was that Khrushchev was catching up with reality.

Stalin had stamped his image on an epoch. This is no place to argue whether Stalinism was inevitable or Stalin necessary. I myself believe that neither Lenin nor Stalin was inevitable or necessary, that it would have been possible for Russia to complete her industrial revolution, educate a nation of illiterate peasants, and turn herself into a great industrial power second to none by gentler and more democratic means. But she did not. Stalin and Stalinism existed, and the society which Stalin created owed its existence to him and was run by men who were nothing but his creatures. He and they, however, outlived their usefulness. Having created a highly articulated society with its multitudinous skills and conflicting interests, Stalin did not know what to do with it and he was temperamentally incapable of giving it its head, or, indeed, the least freedom for initiative and enterprise. So that his new society, ruled draconically by terror, suffered from moral and intellectual paralysis. He had called into being the machinery and the skills to work the machinery, but he treated as mindless helots the men and women in whom he had instilled these skills. As a consequence, at the time of his death the whole vast machine was in danger of total breakdown: only in certain selected enclaves concerned with science as applied to armaments, above all nuclear physics, were the possessors of the requisite skills allowed to exercise all their faculties, to be full men.

What Stalin's successors had to do, and most urgently, was to bring the country alive by allowing it to breathe. They had three main things to contend with: first the enormously powerful vested interests of all those, above all the police, but also entrenched Party functionaries and industrial managers who were used to treating the workers like serfs, with a strong interest in the preservation of the *status quo*; then the pent-up demands of millions who, kept down by rigid terror, would inevitably respond to the slightest relaxation of tyranny by asking for more, both in the way of freedom and in the way of material goods and services; then the catastrophic state of agriculture, which, at the time of Stalin's death, was still producing less than it had done in 1928, before the collectivization – although half the population was still on the land, and although the total population to be fed had been increased by tens of millions.

Everything followed from this. The progress was obscured by the twists and turns which were a direct result of the bitter struggle for personal power between Stalin's heirs. It was made more difficult because of yet another legacy of Stalin's, the cold war and the consequent virtual isolation of the Soviet Union combined with a crippling burden of armaments, which had developed as a result of Stalin's post-war expansionist policies. It was made more urgent because once it had broken the power of the police the new leadership had no authority in itself. Stalin had been his own authority. But who, once absolute terror was renounced, was Malenkov? Who Khrushchev? Who Molotov? What right had any or all of them to rule? In their speeches they presented themselves as the natural heirs of Lenin, the only Bolshevik who stood in the eyes of the people for anything at all. But in their behaviour they appealed directly to the people: unless they could win the people, ruthlessly oppressed for decades, they were doomed. The people in this context included the army, headed then by Marshal Zhukov, brought back from the obscurity into which he had been cast by Stalin.

Progress was made. More and more strongly Khrushchev emerged as the man who stood for progress. More and more

Malenkov and Molotov were manoeuvred into the background. Until, in February 1956, Khrushchev felt strong enough to make his great gamble and present himself in person as the man who was prepared to jettison the whole apparatus of Stalinism and lead the country towards the light. While condemning his late master he so contrived things that some of the mud he threw at Stalin splashed his own most dangerous rivals. He also performed a remarkable conjuring trick: while presenting himself as the true heir of Lenin, bringing the Soviet Union back to the straight and narrow path after years of hideous aberration, he contrived, as we have seen, to emasculate certain doctrines of the great founder.

After that there was no looking back. For a few months in the autumn of 1956 and early 1957 it seemed that Khrushchev was about to be destroyed by the pent-up forces he had set free, when Poland defied the Moscow government, when the Hungarian rebellion had to be put down by Soviet troops, when throughout the Soviet Union students found courage to demonstrate openly against government restrictions and workers to strike for a better life; but by the summer of 1957 he had ridden the storm and, with the active help of the army leader, Zhukov, crushed the opposition. The ruling apparatus of the Communist Party was now subservient to him, and a few months later Khrushchev was able to use that apparatus to secure the downfall of Marshal Zhukov himself, to whom he owed so much, but who, with Malenkov and Molotov defeated, now represented the only actual threat to his authority.

Nevertheless, Khrushchev was not another Stalin. He had triumphed, and he was the supreme leader. But whereas Stalin had created his own ruling élite, raising from nothing to positions of power countless individuals, who thus owed everything to him and to whom he owed nothing, Khrushchev was himself largely the creation of his own supporters: they had raised him up and they could break him. He was, in a word, dictator by consent. And throughout his tenure of office, or reign, he has had to pay constant attention to the voices, the demands, of others.

The sort of society which Khrushchev is trying to build, his successes and failures, his methods, I have written about elsewhere.* It is enough to say here that he is primarily concerned with turning Stalin's prison-house into a prosperous modern society materially as rich, or richer, than the United States, and morally her superior. This has to be done not by giving every individual his head and seeing what happens, with the minimum of interference by the central government, but by detailed prescription from above, with the individual permitted just enough freedom of choice to engage his active participation – but no more. The central government seeks to operate through a chosen élite of party functionaries, the ruling apparatus; but although indoctrination in the theories of Marx and Engels, as amended first by Lenin, then by Khrushchev himself, still looms large in the training of this élite, and although in the course of that indoctrination a great deal of stress is laid on the absolute opposition between capitalism and Communism, and the ultimate triumph of the latter in global revolution, this does not amount *in practice* to much more than that Soviet Communists, and, through them, the whole of Soviet youth, are taught to think about the non-Communist world in a certain way – as the enemy always seeking the overthrow of the Soviet Union, to be worked against by all possible means, the exterior cause of all the hardships suffered by the Soviet people; but an enemy who is foredoomed. *In practice* this way of thinking, though much more systematically induced, is not fundamentally different from the way of thinking which governs the West – namely that Communism is the enemy, always seeking the overthrow of the West, to be worked against by all possible means, the exterior cause of the immense burden of armaments – an enemy, however, who will triumph if we don't watch out.

I am not here discussing the relative truth of these two mirror attitudes. I am only concerned with their effect on Soviet and Western society. Russia is more active in subversion than, for example, America; various bourgeois countries tolerate the existence of Communist Parties, working as fifth columns for Russia, whereas no Communist country tolerates the existence of a capitalist party. All this, and more besides, is true. But these extra-mural activities must be seen as specialist aspects of high

* Most recently in *Khrushchev's Russia* (Pelican).

governmental policy in the international arena. They affect the lives, the thinking, the interest of the ordinary Party functionary no more than the activities of the C.I.A. affect the lives, the thinking, the interest of the ordinary American (less indeed, because the international pursuits of the Soviet Communist Party are far more secretly conducted than those of the C.I.A.). And just as we live and conduct our own society for its own sake, seeing in the Soviet Union no more than a standing external threat, so the Russians, including all but the most relevantly specialized of Party functionaries, pursue their own lives and concentrate on the development of their own society, seeing in the West no more than a standing threat to the unfolding of that development. Russians today are patriots brought up to think of the capitalist countries as the enemy; they are not, save for a highly specialized few thousands out of more than 200 millions, remotely concerned with international Communism, or with capitalism except as a dirty word.

In their own domestic affairs their detachment from what we think of as the Communist ideology is even more complete. The international activities of the Communist Party of the Soviet Union (that small part of it concerned with international affairs) do still, if in a highly dilute measure, reflect Leninist principles. Its domestic activities do nothing of the kind. The idealism which inspired Lenin, even as his intolerant megalomania drove him to construct the system and to institute the Terror which was to cripple it, was killed stone-dead by Stalin. By the middle 1930s the survivors of the revolutionary idealists were all quite literally killed. Their places were taken by Stalin's creatures, and all that was required from the people they governed was perfect obedience and unquestioning acceptance. Any form of idealism was anathema to Stalin. Any individual who really believed in Lenin's ideals was bound, sooner or later, to start asking questions. So he was put away. After some decades of this behaviour the very idea of Communism, in the eyes of the Soviet people, became synonymous with tyranny, privilege, and corruption. The Communist Party at the time of Stalin's death – then some six million strong, was 'they'; the people were 'us'. One day a friend of mine talking to an intelligent peasant on a remote collective asked how many Communists there were in that village: 'Communists?' the man replied. 'Communists, my goodness! You won't find any of those round here. We're all poor!'

But idealism will not die. It survived under Stalin in the hearts of millions, coming out in the most remarkable ways. It attached itself to dreams of a better, happier Soviet Union, of a great country which would be worthy of all the frustrated virtues of the Russian people. But it recognized no body of doctrine, and it looked not to the apparatus of the Communist Party but to individual effort and example one day to overcome the dead weight of 'them'. Many who were moved by some sort of idealism found it convenient to join the Party (but rarely to become its professional functionaries), or attached themselves to it because the only possible path to improvement, short of another revolution, seemed to them to lie through the internal regeneration of the Party. This did not mean that Communism, as practised by Stalin, was for them a creed. At the other end of the scale, simple people in their millions, who saw the Party as the source of all woe, developed a kind of mystique about Stalin, so clearly a gigantic figure in the grand Russian tradition of stern despots, and saw him as a rough but benevolent father-figure cut off from his people by a corrupt and tyrannical army of Communist functionaries, the sources of all evil. The result was a muddle.

Idealism found an outlet in the great war against Germany. It was love of country – my country right or wrong – and this burning patriotism was carefully exploited by Stalin. What started as the Imperialist War between Britain, France, and Poland against Nazi Germany, became the Great Patriotic War when Germany invaded Russia. This newly articulated patriotism survived the renewed bitterness of Stalin's last phase, and was ready to blossom in a thousand ways when Stalin died. It stood now not for defeating the Germans, not for continuing to bear with the Kremlin's arbitrary rule for the sake of a remote future, but for the immediate realization of the dream that had for so long been denied. Any man with less authority than Stalin who tried to rule the Soviet Union after Stalin's death in Stalin's way would have been cast out. Stalin's successors, whether they wanted to or not, had to loosen the rein; and very soon it was clear that the supreme succession would go to the man who was most skilled at promising much and giving just enough to maintain his own authority while keeping firm control. That man was Khrushchev. And Khrushchev's first tasks at home were to provide more food, more houses, more consumer goods without wrecking the basis of the economy, to allow freedom enough for people to begin to realize their full potentialities, without inviting anarchy; his first task abroad was to arrive at some sort of *modus vivendi* with the West which would give the Soviet Union breathing time not only to set her own house in order but also to transform the European satellites from a group of oppressed colonies into a self-respecting circle of loyal allies. At the same time he conceived it to be in the interests of the Soviet Union to continue to make life as difficult as possible as cheaply as possible for the 'imperialist' powers, in order to weaken the grand Western alliance. One way of doing this was to ensure that the ex-colonial nations, the neutralists, the un-committed, were kept out of the imperialist camp, even though this meant Soviet support and aid for violently anti-Communist regimes: Khrushchev did not mind their being anti-Communist, provided they were anti-American too. In this he showed more sense, and a more acute sense of contemporary reality, than many Americans. He reversed Lenin's attitude, 'he who is not for me is against me', into a variant of his own, 'he who is not against me is for me', or, better still, 'he who is against the United States is for the Soviet Union'. Too many American politicians gave him comfort by echoing this attitude, oblivious of the fact that they were playing into Khrushchev's hands.

None of all this has much to do with militant Communism. What it has to do with is the development of Soviet prosperity at home and the strengthening of her position as a power.

What Khrushchev's ultimate aims, what his real hopes, may be we do not know. It is improbable that he sees himself as the Communist overlord of a planet ruled by Communist govern-ments looking to Moscow for instructions. It is possible that he looks forward to the day when the power of finance capital is finally broken in the West, and, with it, the power of adventurist pressure groups operating on government institutions, such as the Pentagon. It is hard to see what more he can expect. But his ultimate aims, conventionally expressed in cheery phrases of a vagueness remarkable even in a professional politician (e.g. 'We shall bury you!') do not concern us here. Khrushchev is a Soviet politician, the first political boss ever to hold power in Russia, concerned above all to make things work and to conserve his own power: as such, he has not much time to sit brooding over ultimate aims. In any case, what concerns us all, and the Chinese too, is not what he vaguely hopes will happen one day, but his immediate conduct; and about his immediate conduct the Chinese are right and we are wrong. It has very little to do with militant Leninism and a great deal to do with the glory and prosperity of the Soviet Union.

He himself has equated, in so many words, Communism with abundance – abundance first for the Soviet Union. And in one of his more remarkable utterances (July 1962) he said:

Communism gives man supreme moral and political satisfaction. But that alone, as you yourselves realize, is not enough. A man may be content with moral and political factors today, tomorrow, and the day after tomorrow, let us say. But after that he may well start to say it would be a good thing to couple moral and political satisfaction with an abundance of meat, milk, butter, and other products. That is right, for without increasing the output of material values in society it will be hard to advance the cause.

What cause?

The Chinese mean something when they speak of the cause, and the cause, as they see it, is not best served by the *embourgeoisement* of the Soviet Union and the fraternization of American presidents and the First Secretary of the Soviet Communist Party. Tightening their belts, they are not amused by certain of Khrushchev's jollier remarks – as for example (in 1959): 'We are getting richer, and when a person has more to eat he gets more democratic.'

Chapter Five

DIFFERENT COUNTRIES:
DIFFERENT WAYS

I

THE Soviet Union has made her revolution, propelled herself into the twentieth century, created a complex society with a vast bourgeoisie and a still vaster proletariat out of a mass of illiterate peasants, consolidated herself as one of the two greatest powers in the world – all this at the cost of infinite suffering. The Soviet people now want to relax; to develop their own interests and explore their own culture; to forget about the revolutionary struggle. Forty-six years is a long time. Very few of the senior Party functionaries of today played any part in the revolution: most of them were infants when it took place. For the great army of the young the collectivization, the first five-year plans, the great purges themselves, are history. A young Soviet Communist today, beginning to make a career, twenty-five years old and with the world at his feet, was born in 1938. Then the great purge was being brought to an end. The Molotov–Ribbentrop Pact lay a year ahead. For him the days of Stalin's final victory are as remote as Munich for his contemporary in England; the collectivization as remote as the formation of Ramsay Macdonald's National Government; the October Revolution as remote as Passchendaele. This is a thing we tend to forget.

But China is situated quite differently. Her revolution is only fifteen, not forty-five, years old. Her government has still not been recognized by the United States and still plays no part in the United Nations. By a strict chronological comparison she stood, when disagreement with the Soviet Union became unmanageable in 1960, where the Soviet Union had stood in the first year of the first five-year plan, a year after the expulsion of Trotsky, a year before the civil war against the peasants which was called the collectivization.

Whereas the Soviet Union is relaxing in comparative affluence and increasingly aware of herself as one great country among others, China is still in the stage of struggle and bitter privation, fighting in almost total isolation to realize her own utopian dreams and at the same time conscious of a deep moral responsibility to other lands which have scarcely begun the struggle – conscious, too, it goes without saying, of her frustrated status as a great power.

There is something in this sort of comparison. It was made to me by Russians in private, long before the quarrel crystallized out. 'The Chinese seem to be making all the same mistakes that we made in the thirties', a Soviet functionary murmured to me as far back as 1955, 'plus a great many of their own. And all on a far greater scale. If only they would learn from our mistakes!' It has been made often enough by Western commentators on the Sino–Soviet scene. The implication is that one day the Chinese also will emerge into comparative affluence, forget about the revolutionary struggle, and concentrate on bourgeois comforts. On being Chinese? Then it will be some other country's turn. . . .

But although there is something in it, this out-of-stepness, this chronological discrepancy or time-lag, is very far from being the whole explanation of the ideological differences between the two countries – and, of course, it does not account for the inter-State differences in any way at all.

The Communist Party of the Soviet Union, the one-time Bolshevik wing of the Russian Social Democratic Party led by Lenin, achieved power and consolidated it in an extremely idiosyncratic way. It did not make the Russian revolution. This was made in March 1917 by the people of Russia, above all as represented by the workers of Petrograd and garrison troops, rising in desperation against autocracy and causing the Tsar to abdicate. At this time the population of Russia was some 130 million. There were 76,000 Bolsheviks. By far the largest revolutionary party was the Social Revolutionary Party, an essentially peasant party. None of the Bolshevik leaders was in Petrograd or Moscow. Lenin was in Switzerland; Trotsky, who at that time was not a Bolshevik, was in Canada. Stalin, Kamenev, and many others were in exile in Siberia. The senior member of the Bolshevik party then in Petrograd was Vyacheslav Scribian, *alias*

Molotov, who was then a bespectacled and stammering young man of twenty-seven, a wholly unknown figure compared with the Menshevik elders Dan, Martov, Chkeidzke, Tseretelli, and the Social Revolutionaries, Kerensky and Chernov.

Lenin got back to Russia in the famous sealed train in April. He had nothing but contempt for the revolution as it had developed and for the Provisional Government which was seeking to establish a democratic society. Instead of cooperating with his fellow-revolutionaries in an attempt to create a new order out of chaos he stood apart, drawing his fellow Bolsheviks with him, using every art of unscrupulous demagogy and chicanery to turn the peasants and the workers against the new administration, which really fell because it tried to honour its war-time obligations to Britain and France. The October revolution was not a revolution of a popular kind: it was a *Putsch*, a desperate gamble by a minority revolutionary party, controlling certain strategically placed regiments of dissident troops, which involved using force against the first democratic government in Russian history. There were then 240,000 Bolsheviks: the party had tripled its membership in seven months. To preserve appearances Lenin had to go through with the elections to the new Constituent Assembly, the symbol of all that the liberals and revolutionaries of Russia had striven towards for so long. But in spite of manipulation in the now familiar Communist manner the elections went heavily against the Bolsheviks: 370 seats went to the right-wing Social Revolutionaries; 40 to the left wing of that party; only 175 to the Bolsheviks, and 124 to other parties, including the Mensheviks. Lenin's answer was to station troops round the building when the Assembly met in January 1918 and dissolve it. This was the beginning and the end of the first democratic parliament in Russian history. Soon after that Lenin proscribed all opposition parties and created the Cheka, an instrument of Terror, the first incarnation of that celebrated *corps d'élite* which was later to be known as the G.P.U., the N.K.V.D., and the M.G.B. It was modelled on the Tsarist *Ochrana*, the scourge of all revolutionaries and liberals, and it was to serve later on as the model for the Gestapo. In due course the Russian people, who had made the revolution, not helped by the Bolsheviks, in March 1917, began to realize that the man into whose safekeeping they had entrusted the fruits of their great achievement had, not to put too fine a point on it, betrayed them. They began to protest. Chief among the protesters were the sailors of the Kronstadt naval base, who had been outstanding among the revolutionary fighters. Lenin had them shot down, operating through Trotsky; and that was the end of organized popular rebellion. The year was 1921, when the Bolsheviks had been able to consolidate their power largely because they proved their discipline and worth in providing a hard centre of resistance to the armies of the White Russians, backed by the Western powers and feared and hated by the peasants, as dispossessed land-owners seeking to recover their lost estates. So they fought with the Red Army for their newly won land and were victorious – only to find a few years later that Stalin wanted their land.

The point of all this is that the Bolsheviks won Russia by trickery, demagogy, and the skilled manipulation of elemental forces. Having won it, they held it by terror.

This was the universal rule. At no time was there any serious attempt to persuade the opposition, only to trick it or frighten it into subjection. When, in 1922, after the civil war, the inter-vention, and the appalling famine, Lenin had to retreat and introduce his New Economic Policy in order to get the economy working again, he still did not try to persuade. He simply invited all those who felt inclined to take the risk to set up, within the framework of the Soviet State, a limited free-enterprise economy, with the incentive of quick profits. Some of the best elements in Russia threw themselves into the N.E.P. experiment because they hoped it was the beginning of a more liberal system. The more intelligent of the worst elements joined in too in order to get rich quickly. Many of the best among the Bolsheviks were humiliated and shamed by this cynical manoeuvring. But no attempt whatsoever was made to convert these people to a Communist, or Socialist, outlook. They were simply used, regarded by Lenin with contempt, to be thrown away when they had fulfilled their function.

Lenin died in 1924, and it was Stalin who threw them away in 1928. By that time the practice of ruling through the police was firmly established. Stalin was not interested in what people thought, only in what they said and did. One of the most remarkable things about Bolshevik rule from the beginning until the death of Stalin thirty-seven years later was the conspicuous absence of any attempt to convert sceptics or opponents to the Leninist view of life. From the beginning the survivors of the pre-revolutionary bourgeoisie were excluded, for a long time their children after them. Virtually the only exceptions to this rule were a number of Tsarist army officers who threw in their lot with the Red Army: these, of course, were subject to army discipline. Once Stalin took over in 1924 he seems to have operated on the principle that the only thing to do with the middle-aged and the responsibly minded young was to jettison them, using them up until they were worn out in his vast labour-camps. Those who submitted utterly to the discipline of Party and police might find a place in society. Those who were honest enough or brave enough to ask questions were treated as scrap.

It may be asked how this account may be reconciled with what is known of the vast apparatus of propaganda, the work of countless party agitators on every level throughout the country, the endless compulsory lectures on Marxist-Leninism. In fact the reconciliation is quite easy. The Soviet propaganda apparatus in all its ramifications has never been concerned with persuasion, only with instruction. There is all the difference in the world between arguing with sceptics and seeking to persuade them on the one hand and, on the other, simply telling them, endlessly and inescapably, what to think. The one is an affair of enlightenment; the other of intimidation: think this, or *say* you think this, or else . . .

Even when it came to the children, who, so Stalin imagined, could be educated in a certain manner of thinking more easily than their elders, their political indoctrination though formidable in extent was perfunctory in depth. Again, they were never educated in Marxist-Leninism as a vital faith. They were taught certain facts and attitudes, as children in this country were once taught to learn by heart the names of the rivers of Europe, or the catechism. The surfaces of their minds were moulded to take the line of least resistance; what lay below the surface was un-nourished and untouched. The political instructors, more often than not, were either school-teachers who themselves had been forced to learn by heart texts from Marx, Lenin, and Stalin which they scarcely comprehended, or by barely literate workers and peasants, turned junior Party agitators, who did not even know that there was anything to comprehend. For them the text was all. 'God is love'; 'a little child shall lead them'; 'vengeance is mine', saith the Lord, 'I will repay'. It was all in the day's work. This is the wrong set of texts, but never mind.

2

How different was all this from the Chinese revolutionary experience. After the false start and corruption of Sun Yat-sen's revolution the Chinese Communist Party, founded in 1921, became the unified force which we know today. Before he became the undisputed leader Mao Tse-tung himself conducted at least one purge of dissident colleagues. Hundreds of thousands, almost certainly more than a million non-Communists, were killed in the Land Reform. All in all, it seems that the Chinese Communists have behaved no less cruelly than the Russians. But the fact remains that from 1927 onwards the party which swept Mao into power in 1948, and still sustains him, was, beginning with a mere handful of men, an organically developing force, led by men who had worked and thought together for many years. Certainly when Mao's revolution triumphed and Chiang Kai-shek was finally broken, his Communist Party membership amounted to only a tiny fraction of the immense population of China. But, unlike Lenin's Bolshevik Party, it did not have to use trickery to conquer: it was the most powerful coherent force in China, and it beat Chiang's army in a straight fight. It also achieved power by fighting towards the centre from the periphery, whereas Lenin had to conquer all Russia from the centre.

It was led, moreover, by men who had been working and fighting together for twenty years, men approaching or past fifty. All had been steeled by long, active periods of underground resistance; most had commanded revolutionary armies, or had long experience in administering Communist-held territory, or both. Mao himself was fifty-four in 1948.

In 1917 Lenin had been forty-seven, and for many years had lived and worked abroad. Trotsky was thirty-eight, and so was

Stalin. Zinoviev was thirty-four and so was Kamenev. None of these men, or any of their colleagues (many still younger), had the least experience of administration, of leading armies. None had even begun to think about problems of government. They were a disciplined set of revolutionary conspirators who had spent most of their adult lives in exile in Russia or abroad. Lenin, their natural leader, had nothing but contempt for problems of government: he proposed to find his administrators among bakers and candle-stick makers: all they had to do was to carry out the orders that he himself would give them. All except Lenin, an opportunist politician of genius, Trotsky, an extraordinary combination of the demagogue and the man of action, and Stalin himself were professional revolutionary intellectuals who knew nothing about life and nothing about people. In due course Stalin came to the top and killed off the intellectuals, replacing them with the Khrushchevs and the Kaganoviches and a host of tough boss-types of proletarian and peasant origin. Fifteen years after the revolution these new men were for all practical purposes supreme. And they were all young. Fifteen years after Mao's revolution, in spite of a number of purges, his original band of revolutionary fighters, nearly all of them of bourgeois or prosperous peasant origin, and well educated, were still in charge – as they are to this day – most of them now in their sixties with forty years of unbroken tradition and responsibility behind them.

This is one of the fundamental differences between the Soviet and the Chinese ruling class, as they now stand opposed. A powerful group of veterans, for forty years masters of their own fate, for fifteen years masters of their country, which they conquered by their own unaided efforts, are not in the best of times going to look kindly on a group of Russian parvenus, who took no part in any revolution, who were the creatures of Stalin, or those creatures' creatures. They are certainly not going to take any orders from them.

There is another aspect of the Chinese revolution which is frequently overlooked. As we have seen, from the beginning Lenin relied on trickery, on force, not caring what the people thought so long as they obeyed. Force has also been used with the utmost freedom by Mao and his colleagues, and their victims number millions. But whereas once they had seized power, and perhaps indeed because they represented such an insignificant minority in Russia, the Bolsheviks were content with force, the Chinese experience has been very different. From the beginning very great stress was laid on persuasion and conversion, 'reconstruction'. There is no need here to enter into a discussion on the meaning and efficacy of brainwashing – a catch-phrase, the loose use of which has done us untold harm, as all phrases which obscure reality must do harm. The point to be made is that the Chinese Communists consistently went out of their way to bring their opponents round to their own way of thinking – not by indiscriminate use of the Russian indoctrination techniques, but by genuine, perhaps misguided, perhaps naïve, perhaps downright cruel, efforts to transform the mind of the individual, who, if he responded, was ensured a decent place in the new Communist society. Thus talents which in the Soviet Union would have been roughly destroyed were nurtured and used. Still another difference, as a rule not properly appreciated, is the strength in the early days of the Chinese revolution of the educated intelligentsia, the great clerkly caste, who formed a leaven to the peasant masses. Russia in 1917 had no corresponding phalanx.

But the greatest difference of all was that Mao based his strength on the peasants themselves, whereas to Lenin and Stalin they were highly suspect; they were, indeed, the enemy: with ownership of their own land as their only desire, with the stronger ones for ever seeking to augment their holdings at the expense of the weaker brethren, they formed an inert conservative mass, imbued with the petit-bourgeois spirit, who could all too easily wreck the system which Lenin had built by harnessing the urban proletariat. Since the peasants in 1917 accounted for eighty per cent of the population of Russia they made a formidable enemy. They were treated as such. And the result was that, although their active power was finally broken by the enforced collectivization with its massacres, its man-made famine, its deportations of millions of the most able peasant farmers, they remained for decades, as indeed they still remain, a millstone round the neck of the new state, apathetic, uncooperative, unproductive.

Mao was to do terrible things to his Chinese peasants. But in the early days he based his power on them and his armies were peasant armies. When the time came to collectivize them this action was undertaken not as it had been undertaken in Russia, primarily as the means of breaking the spirit of a hostile mass, but in the supposed interests of efficiency.

3

It has to be remembered that Mao and his colleagues were deeply under the spell of the Soviet example. Lenin and his Bolsheviks knew all too little about Russia, but at least they knew something about the outside world in the early days of their new system, even though they viewed its activities through distorting spectacles. The Chinese Communists knew everything about China, nothing at all about the outside world, not much about Russia. Many of them had indeed been to school in the Soviet Union, but there they were cut off from the lives of the Soviet people and, as foreign Communists, were treated, segregated in a kind of limbo, to the only real exercise of reasoned indoctrination that the Russians ever undertook. Russia, when all was said, was the home of the revolution: but her Chinese guests did not know what it was like to live in that home. They knew next to nothing either about Stalin's appalling tyranny or about the growing *embourgeoisement* of the Soviet 'new class' of rulers. So when they began to set up their local administrations in the territory they held, and later when they took over the administration of the whole country and achieved their miracle of centralization in a land torn for so long by rival war-lords, they not unnaturally sought to follow the Soviet example, regardless of how it had actually worked, regardless of the real motives behind Lenin's and Stalin's actions. And, on paper, one of the most striking aspects of the Soviet example was the collectivization of agriculture. The Chinese did not know that it had failed so lamentably that even to this day, and in spite of Khrushchev's frantic plunging to put things right (always within the framework of the collectivization), it was responsible for the chronic lag in Soviet food-production. And so they repeated Stalin's grossest error. It was all very well for my Russian friend to shake his head over this. He should have remembered – perhaps he did not know – that the Russians having made their own great mistake had, twenty years later, forced all their European satellites to repeat that mistake, and that the only Communist country which had undone the collectivization, Poland under Gomulka, was the only Communist country in which agriculture was not a national disgrace.

China is used to famine, to natural disasters of every kind. But the Chinese are also a nation of skilful and industrial intensive farmers, which the Russians have never been. The collectivization failed. Mao at least quickly realized that it had failed, which is more than Stalin ever realized. Khrushchev realized that it had failed, but, unable to admit it, sought to remedy the deficiency by taking in great areas of unused land, the so-called Virgin Lands, to be exploited not by collectives but by a system of ranch-farming centred on vast State farms. China had no unused land. So to remedy the failure of collectivization Mao introduced the system of communes, which was collectivization-plus and its development in logic. The essence of the collective system in agriculture was a variation, or perversion, of a peculiarly Russian system. In its simplest original form the collective was the population of a village. All the lands belonging to the peasants of that village were lumped together and made over to the population of the village in perpetuity to be farmed by communal effort as one unit, directed by an elected or a nominated manager. Livestock and dead-stock were pooled too. Rather than surrender their stock the peasants in their millions slaughtered them, and it was for this reason that the livestock population of the Soviet Union, including draught horses, was reduced by a half between 1928 and 1931. At that time dead-stock meant only hand-tools and horse-drawn ploughs and harrows. There was no machinery to speak of. When machinery began to arrive it was concentrated in the celebrated Machine Tractor Stations, each serving a whole group of collectives and kept under central control. There was more in this idea than economy in the utilization of machinery: the men at the M.T.S.s, who were paid in kind by the collectives, were supposed to act as the eyes of the central authority in its efforts to ensure that the peasants worked properly on the collectives and did not conceal any part of what they had reaped. The peasants themselves were required to put in so many hours a week on the collective land, and the collectives as a whole were required to deliver at an artificially low price a certain fixed amount, according to the Plan, of grain, milk, meat, etc. to the State. The rest they could keep for their own consumption. But often enough they could not even meet their compulsory delivery quota. What enabled them to live was the institution of small private plots, which varied in size from time to time, and the privilege of keeping a cow or two or three pigs or geese on those plots. The products of these plots they were allowed to consume themselves or sell on the open market at prices which were always very much higher than the government price. Because the peasants were not state employees, like the factory workers, but were technically communal landowners, they received no social benefits. Except in very rich areas there was no question of the collective making a profit or providing a decent livelihood for its members. These, therefore, skimped their work on the communal land and concentrated all their efforts on their own private plots, regardless of the country's needs.

This was the system which China, with an entirely different agricultural tradition of small-scale highly intensive farming, saddled itself with in 1955. It made for the worst of both worlds. It provided no incentives for individual effort, and, at the same time, it fell a long way short of streamlined regimentation. The communes were instituted to provide the regimentation, which for a time went to extremes which were farcical as well as tragic: men and women lived, husbands segregated from wives, in barracks. Home life was broken up, and individuals, herded together, were fed, as they worked, in gangs. There was no pretence about this. 'All the ties that bind the peasants are broken. ... The frames of individual families which had existed for thousands of years have been completely smashed,' Pekin radio proudly proclaimed. All for each and each for all, with a vengeance. It was the logical step towards communization which the Russians had never dared take. That was in August 1958. Even before they had been consolidated, the brand-new collective farms, 700,000 of them, had been merged into 26,000 communes, embracing half a million peasants, regimented in what one can only call divisions some 20,000 strong, including their women and children, summoned by bells and whistles at dawn, paraded, marched off to the fields in companies and platoons, each under its commander, bearing flags. They received no pay. They worked for their food, their shelter, their elementary clothing.

This was the system which was in a year or so to industrialize agriculture and do away for ever with the difference between the peasants and the urban workers, also to be organized in communes. The rural communes went hand in hand with the Great Leap Forward, with its slogan 'twenty years of progress concentrated in a single day'. It was the Chinese answer to the Soviet line that no country could build Communism until it had converted its collectives into state farms – a conversion that had lagged in the Soviet Union for a variety of reasons, not least that State employees have to be paid, fed, and provided with social services, all of which costs money, money for investment, and money to pay the urban workers who would suddenly find their food much dearer. It was to show, too, that China could move an agrarian country into Communism without waiting for the completion of her industrial revolution. Three out of four Chinese were still peasants, as compared with one in two in Khrushchev's Russia. And in 1958, the year of the Great Leap Forward, the Soviet Union, after forty years of Communist rule, was still in the stage of Socialism, as the Kremlin saw it – had, indeed, only just achieved that stage (Molotov had recently been attacked for arguing that even that stage had not yet been reached), and had a long way to go before the achievement of Communism. It was not until 1961, as we shall see, that Khrushchev laid down the formal programme for the transition from Socialism to Communism in the Soviet Union, a period of twenty years. In 1958, when he came out with his first attack on the pretension of the Chinese communes, he made it very clear that the Chinese claim was not only nonsensical but positively heretical.

As indeed it was, and dangerously heretical into the bargain. Because the commune system, with its promised short cut to the millennium, untold hardship to lead very swiftly to unimaginable rewards, had a magic vitality which was totally lacking, which for decades had been totally lacking, in the Soviet example. It was all too likely to appeal far more vividly to the backward countries of the world, countries with no industry, knowing only poverty, than the new Soviet model with its stupendous production of oil and steel and sputniks, its teeming technocrats, its colossal state machine. If the underdeveloped countries of Africa and Asia had to follow the Soviet road to achieve a Communist society there was no particular point in their even starting: apart from all other considerations, the Soviet Union was unique in the richness of its natural resources. How was Indonesia to emulate Magnitogorsk? But if she could not achieve Communism through steel and oil, she could do so through communes.

In 1958 the Chinese, of course, were desperate. They had a problem right outside the Soviet experience – an exploding population. And, unlike the Soviet Union, they had no vast reserves of living space and cultivatable land. They were squeezed to the limit. Frantically trying to build up their own industry they saw their population growing ever faster than the food supply. Collectivization on the Soviet model was seen at once not to be the answer. They must go the logical step further, and at once. There seems little doubt that they believed that it would work. In 1958 it was announced that food production would be doubled in a year, and to all appearances they believed it. While at the same time backyard industry, including the local manufacture of steel by primitive methods, would supplement enormously the more conventional methods of production. The whole population was to be mobilized to a crash production plan run on quasi-military lines. And necessity was to be translated into virtue; China would overtake the Soviet Union in the race to Communism.

It was then, for the first time, that Khrushchev threw his wet blanket over the whole enterprise. Using the occasion of the abolition of the Machine Tractor Stations and the announcement of his plan to abolish compulsory deliveries from the collectives and the institution of payment in cash instead of kind, he said – never mentioning the Chinese: 'Some comrades will ask: But if we want to go forward to Communism, how can our path lie through a market economy? ... We have all been taught at school that Communism means organized distribution and no market at all.' He answered his own question: 'We cannot achieve Communism until we have abundance. We cannot have abundance until we lower costs. And we cannot lower costs without the yardstick of the rouble.'

There seems little doubt that by this time, no matter what they may have believed before, the Chinese were beginning to understand where Khrushchev's policies were inevitably tending – away from Communism and towards a managed economy motivated by essentially bourgeois ideals.

Soon Khrushchev was to be more specific about the communes as such, though refraining from attacking the Chinese directly. At the 21st Soviet Party Congress in February 1959 he went out of his way to insist that the collective-farm system, which the Chinese had abandoned, 'serves and can go on serving for a long time the development of the productive forces of agriculture.' And he attacked those people who were trying to rush the introduction of Communist principles of distribution. This sort of premature 'levelling', he said, would not accelerate the transition to Communism but would, instead, discredit Communism. When he spoke at the 21st Party Congress he had already indicated his thoughts about the communes to the world as a whole, including the Chinese, in rather a curious way. In an interview given to the American Senator, Humphries, which he knew would go round the world, he had said in effect that the Soviet Union had once experimented with communes, but only as a temporary measure in the early days of the revolution, in the period of War Communism when everything was in desperately short supply. It was at once plain, he said, that the system would not do, and that without material incentives there could be no question of 'leading the millions forward to Communism'.

Chapter Six

CHINA INTO EUROPE

I

No documents are available to display the precise contours of Chinese thought immediately after the epoch-making Congress, or to tell us whether Mao Tse-tung engaged in any argument with Khrushchev, or with those in Khrushchev's own government, who for one reason or another, opposed him – for example Molotov, who stood against Khrushchev from Stalinist conviction, or Malenkov, then engaged in the bitter struggle for personal power. Nothing was said in public. But that a difference had arisen was at once apparent from the Chinese treatment of Stalin's memory.

From the day of Stalin's burial there had in the Soviet Union been a steady, though not for some time explicit, diminishing of his stature. References to his great achievements became perfunctory, then simply were no more. The Chinese had gone on talking about his greatness with far more insistence than the Russians. But, until 1956, no deep significance could be read into this. After the 20th Congress it was a different matter. In the Soviet Union there was much talk first about Stalin's mistakes, then about his crimes. The Chinese did not join in: they went on talking about him as about a great figure, and although it was allowed that he had not been infallible (this suited Mao's book quite well, for obvious reasons) his mistakes were referred to as small blemishes in a leader of colossal stature. The difference was plain. But at no time did the Chinese publicly challenge the decisions of the 20th Party Congress, and it was not until the Moscow Conference of Communist Parties in November 1957 that they began to question certain implications of Khrushchev's new line of thought.

Much later they were to tax Khrushchev indignantly with his de-Stalinization action, saying that they had not been warned of his intention in advance.[1] But, unless in private, they made no protest at the time.

What they did do very soon was to intervene decisively in the European theatre. One day, when the history of this age comes to be written with detachment, it will be seen that one of Khrushchev's most crucial actions, perhaps the most crucial of all for the world as a whole, was that he brought China into Europe. This happened, almost unremarked by those most closely affected, in the autumn of 1956. It was a direct consequence of the de-Stalinization and it sharply accentuated Chinese reservations about Khrushchev's fitness to lead the world Communist movement.

As everybody knows, the de-Stalinization, coming as a grand climax to a period during which (two steps forward, one backward) the iron discipline maintained by Stalin was progressively relaxed, in eastern and central Europe as well as in the Soviet Union, shook the Communist world, split many of the Communist Parties, undermined the authority of Moscow, including Khrushchev's own authority, and was the direct cause of the revolts first in Poland, then in Hungary. When the Polish revolt flared up and Gomulka, released from prison, took over the new government, Moscow's first reaction was to restore the *status quo* by force. Warsaw was ringed with Soviet tanks; Soviet warships stood off the port of Gdynia; Khrushchev himself, accompanied by Molotov and Malenkov (with whom he was at that time locked in conflict), descended on Warsaw and read the riot act. But the Poles stood firm, and we know now that the Chinese supported them and told the Russians not to use force.[2] Soon Chou En-lai himself flew to Moscow, then to Warsaw, to act as a moderating influence, to explain to the Russians the true inwardness of the Polish revolt, and to explain to Gomulka why he had Chinese support and just how far it would go. We do not know, but it is more than probable, that Khrushchev personally was deeply relieved. He saw his policy of reform on the edge of ruin, and he was under extreme pressure from the Stalinists, headed by Molotov, to revert to the old-fashioned terror. China saved him.

But not for love of Khrushchev. For the next thing that happened was the brutal suppression of the Hungarian revolt, signalized by the reversal of the promise to withdraw Soviet troops and the arrest of Imre Nagy and General Maleter, who had been granted safe-conducts by the Russians in Budapest. It was not until 1960, four years later, that the Chinese announced to the world's Communist Parties that it was under pressure from them that Khrushchev had reversed his decision, broken his word to the leaders of the Hungarian revolt, marched his troops into Budapest, and put down the revolt by force, a claim which is almost certainly only part of the story.

It will be asked at once why in Warsaw the Chinese showed themselves on the side of leniency and a few weeks later, in Budapest, on the side of brute force. The answer to this question is simple. There could be no question of Poland breaking out of the Socialist camp. She was tied to the Soviet Union absolutely, as the sole guarantor of her new frontier with Germany, the Oder–Neisse line. The Gomulka government was a Communist government, and it was in full control of the army. Had the Russians struck there would have been a nasty war which would, in effect, have been a civil war between Communists. Since there was no escape from Poland, blocked from the West by Germany and Czechoslovakia, it was better to reach a compromise solution without a civil war, and this was done. But Hungary was an entirely different case. Here the army had turned against the Communist Party, and the rebels proposed to contract out of the Socialist camp and set up a parliamentary democracy which would adopt an attitude of neutrality between East and West. In a word, Khrushchev in proposing to withdraw Soviet troops was permitting Hungary's defection from the Socialist camp. This was too much for the Chinese. It should be stopped by military action, they insisted, regardless of bloodshed, regardless of appearances. And so it was.

There are a number of interesting points about this sad story. The first is that from the point of view of keeping the Socialist bloc intact the Chinese in both cases showed better judgement than the Russians. A war with the Communist government of Poland, the army at its back, would have been a far more protracted and bloody affair than the suppression of the Hungarian revolt and would have called for a display of ruthlessness, directed against a land ruled by Communists, altogether disproportionate to any conceivable gain. As for Hungary, thanks to sharp military action and a brief and dizzying display of treachery, what was about to be lost was saved.

The second point is that Mao felt strong enough to intervene in Europe, where no Chinese influence had ever been felt before, and Khrushchev felt weak enough to be thankful for this intervention.

The third point is that in the light of China's counsel of moderation in Warsaw and extreme brutality in Budapest, and of Khrushchev's determination to use force in Warsaw followed by his intended retreat from Budapest, we have to be very careful indeed when it comes to sorting out the proponents of a 'soft' line from the proponents of a 'hard' line within the Socialist camp.

2

How was it that Mao came to intervene in two theatres far remote from China or any sphere of past Chinese influence – in Poland and in Hungary, which had been treated by Stalin as though these ancient and proud countries were his private property?

Looking back in the light of the Sino–Soviet conflict as it has since developed, it is easy to see what I myself apprehended only mistily at the time (I saw no more than that Mao was irritated by the manner and extent of the de-Stalinization, and that this was one more item to add to the chronic, scarcely acknowledged friction between Moscow and Pekin), namely that the Chinese had been irritated by Khrushchev's taking so much on himself at the 20th Party Congress and had decided, at a convenient opportunity, to demonstrate to him that he was of lesser calibre than Stalin, that they did not propose to accept him as Stalin's successor in the sense of being undisputed head of the world-wide Communist movement, and that everything that happened inside the Communist world was of vital concern to all Communists everywhere – that if other Parties allowed Moscow to make unilateral decisions for the bloc as a whole without insisting on their voices being heard that was their look-out: China, for her part, insisted on her rights. They could not have asked for a better opportunity to assert this view. With Khrushchev fighting for survival against Molotov and the neo-Stalinists, in alliance with Malenkov, his dedicated foe, there was for a short time almost total confusion in the Kremlin; and both sides could only welcome demonstrative support from Pekin at a moment when the whole European empire was bursting into flames.

Once it is seen how China was determined to assert her rights as a responsible and extremely powerful member of the Communist International, which Stalin had almost succeeded in reducing to a Muscovite colonial system, we can look back beyond 1956. Indeed, we must. Mao was doing in Europe only what Khrushchev had already done in Asia.

In 1955, after Malenkov had been deposed from the premiership and Khrushchev as First Secretary of the Communist Party (with Bulganin, nominal Prime Minister, as a sort of foil, or feeder) was beginning to have things his own way, there took place the celebrated tour of India and Burma, during which Khrushchev went about trying to exploit anti-British, anti-American feeling, deriding the imperialists whom the Indians and Burmese had driven out of their lands, and, in general, turning the occasion into an anti-colonial three-ring circus. It was on this tour that the phrase 'we shall bury you', 'you' being the capitalist world, was first happily coined. And the Western press, very naturally, was much taken up with it. But at the time I suggested publicly that Khrushchev was doing two things at once: certainly he was appealing as strongly as he knew how to anti-colonial feeling everywhere and to anti-British feeling in the Indian sub-continent; but he was also staging a demonstration, I thought and said, against Chinese pretensions in Asia.

This was a guess, or a deduction if that makes it look better; but it was almost certainly an accurate guess, as far as it went. Certainly Khrushchev was serving notice on Mao that Russia's interest in Asia was no less than China's, and that he was not going to tolerate any division of the world into Communist spheres of influence. But he was doing more than this. He was announcing his intention of wooing, with flattery and material aid, the established governments of all those countries which had recently won independence, even though they might be anti-Communist. The government of Nehru was a classic example of what is known to the Communist world as a bourgeois nationalist regime. It was anti-British imperialist (anti-American imperialist too), but only because it stood for an independent India. In no other sense was it a revolutionary government, and its institutions owed much to ideals of parliamentary democracy working within a capitalistic framework. It was markedly anti-Communist. The conventional Leninist attitude to all governments of this kind, whose revolutionary aims were satisfied with the winning of national independence, was that they consisted of 'lackeys of imperialism', who were to be overthrown by true revolutionaries at the first opportunity. Khrushchev's visit to India marked the beginning of a reversal of this attitude (Stalin was far more Leninist than is commonly supposed, very much more so than Khrushchev): he indicated that he was prepared to lavish time, energy, and treasure on providing material and moral support to any government, no matter how anti-Communist, which could be expected to remain neutral in the cold war. The old slogan 'he who is not for me is against me' was conveniently forgotten; from 1955 onward any country could qualify as an object of Soviet solicitude provided only that it kept itself out of the Western camp.

The Chinese were later to attack Khrushchev most sharply for this, for shoring up rotten anti-Communist regimes such as Nasser's Egypt and Soekarno's Indonesia, as well as Nehru's India, and for lavishing on them material and technical aid which honest revolutionaries, such as the Chinese, themselves most desperately needed. Khrushchev's reply to this particular charge of betrayal was that he despised Nehru as much as Mao did; that Nehru, nevertheless, should be supported, since he was keeping India out of the clutches of the imperialists. But what kind of support was it? he demanded, speaking particularly of Nehru. And he answered himself by quoting Lenin: 'We support them as the rope supports the hanged man.'[3]

In fact, the Chinese had a very bad case when, years later, they made this criticism. So bad that, as with certain other of their charges against Khrushchev, one can only conclude that they were desperately searching for doctrinal grounds to cover their detestation of Khrushchev as an unreliable ally, as the man who was prepared to do a deal with an American president in their despite, who refused to put atomic arms at their disposal, who refused to back them actively in the matter of the off-shore islands, and who took India's part against them.

As we shall see, so much of Pekin's criticism of Moscow was, in fact, retrospective. In the very year that Khrushchev and Bulganin were demonstrating in India that the Soviet Union, as a power, was not prepared to regard Asia as a Chinese sphere of influence – a demonstration that had nothing to do with ideology, but only with power politics – Khrushchev was also busily engaged in the wooing of Marshal Tito.

When Khrushchev and Bulganin undertook their pilgrimage to Belgrade in the high summer of 1955 (it was the first time that either man had ever been outside the Soviet Union), the main criticism of Khrushchev's policy came from Molotov. Molotov did not object to the resumption of State relations between the Soviet Union and Yugoslavia, which had been so roughly broken off in 1948; what he objected to was Khrushchev's attempt to re-establish fraternal Party relations between the Communist Party of the Soviet Union and the Yugoslav League of Communists. No doubt there were individual Chinese Communists who felt as Molotov did. But they did not make their voices heard. Even when just a year later, in June 1956, and in the full flood of the post-20th-Party-Congress relaxation, which was soon to lead to the Polish and Hungarian revolts, Khrushchev took a bold step forward in his relations with Yugoslavia, the Chinese made no objection.

Tito had snubbed Khrushchev in Belgrade, accepting as his due the re-opening of State relations, but refusing absolutely to abandon certain of his heretical attitudes which kept him out of the Party fold, or in any way to subordinate his own party to the dictates of the Moscow Central Committee. Now Khrushchev tried again. He invited Tito to Moscow, fêted him expansively, and at the close of the visit allowed to be published a declaration in which, for the first time, inter-Party relations between Belgrade and Moscow were referred to – thus giving practical expression to the new thesis of 'different roads to Socialism' which had been put forward at the Congress itself in February of that year. The Moscow communiqué signed by the Soviet Union and Yugoslavia stated explicitly not only that 'the roads to Socialist development in different countries in different conditions are different', but also that 'diversity in the development of Socialism helps to strengthen it' and that, as far as Moscow and Belgrade were concerned, 'neither one side nor the other has any inclination to impose on others its own conceptions in determining ways and means of Socialist development'.

The Chinese did not object. Indeed, how could they? They themselves were still living under the influence of the spirit of Bandung, and Mao had insisted often enough that his way was different from the Russian way. But this complaisance of Pekin is of first importance in sorting out the origins and real meanings of the Sino–Soviet conflict as it developed. In years to come the Yugoslav way was to symbolize all that was rotten and heretical in Khrushchev's policies. The Chinese were to inveigh against Tito and his revisionism when they were really attacking Khrushchev. It was easy enough to see why. Yugoslavia had refused to join the Socialist camp, had objected to the division of the world into two opposed blocs, had, indeed, accepted economic and military aid from the imperialist camp, was preaching heresies enormously attractive to some of the more sophisticated Parties both inside the bloc and outside – notably the Poles and the Italians – and was actively engaged in trying to rally the neutralists into combining to make some sort of a third force.

But though this is easy to understand, it is not the way the Chinese saw things in 1956. And the fact that they made no protest throughout the critical period from the de-Stalinizing 20th Party Congress in February 1956 to the Moscow Conference of Communist Parties in 1957 was to weaken, indeed to undermine, the whole of the imposing ideological edifice they began to build up in 1958: either they had failed abysmally in prescience, which could not be admitted, or they were cheating when, later, they were to say that they had objected to Khrushchev's policies ever since the 20th Party Congress. In fact they failed in foresight and they cheated into the bargain. They may well have had reservations – indeed, it is clear that they did – about Khrushchev's handling of the memory of Stalin. But against his revolutionary theses they made no protest at all.

The whole period really was one of general confusion. Long

before Pekin's opposition to Khrushchev's policies crystallized
into a counter-policy of its own there must have been a great
deal of fairly heated debate inside the Chinese Politburo. And
it is this confusion which makes it impossible to decide just how
the Chinese opposition developed. The Soviet Union itself was
confused. After the shock of the de-Stalinization Khrushchev
was fighting for survival against some of his closest colleagues.
The Chinese were trying to adapt themselves to the changed
situation. And indeed throughout the world-Communist movement nobody quite knew what was going to happen next, or even
what was wanted next. Among the livelier fraternal Parties,
Togliatti in Rome was beginning to make the running, which he
kept up ever after, with his invention of the theory of 'poly-
centrism' – calling for a union of virtually autonomous Communist Parties, as opposed to the monolithic bloc system
centrally controlled by Moscow. Togliatti, moreover, very
boldly attacked the Moscow leadership – that is Khrushchev
himself – for ascribing all the evils exposed at the 20th Party
Congress to Stalin personally, when in fact, he argued, at least
some of these evils must have been inherent in the Soviet system
itself. Other Parties, or factions, were also taking this line –
among them, though in a fairly subdued way, the Chinese
themselves.

The confusion, which came to a head in the autumn of 1956
with the Polish and Hungarian revolts, persisted until the very
eve of the Moscow Conference of November 1957. By that time,
after coming within an inch of total overthrow in the spring of
1957, Khrushchev had collected all his force and smashed his
domestic opposition, symbolized by the anti-Party group, a
factitious alliance of men as widely apart as Molotov and
Malenkov, who had united only for the purpose of bringing
Khrushchev down. In the autumn he felt ready to convene a
conference of all the Communist Parties. The Communist
movement as a whole had begun to settle once more on an even
keel, and Khrushchev's sole aim was to reassert Moscow's
authority – his own personal authority – after a period of
dissonance and strain. The Chinese backed him up to the hilt.
The Conference ended with a formal declaration of Communist
policy, in which the leading role of the Soviet Union was

emphasized, and which carried heavy warnings against those parties who might carry poly-centrism too far. Confusion seemed to be clarified – but not at all. Moscow and Pekin thought they understood each other, and the Moscow Declaration was based on this belief. They were wrong.

Chapter Seven

THE MOSCOW DECLARATION, 1957

I

THE Moscow Conference of November 1957 appeared on the face of it to be a routine affair – admittedly on a rather grand scale – concerned above all with the mending of fences after the upheavals of 1956 and the savage internecine warfare which ended in Khrushchev's defeat of the anti-Party group and his triumph over the very peculiar, *ad hoc* alliance between Malenkov, Molotov, and Kaganovich. It was indeed precisely this. But it was also something more. It marked the watershed of Sino–Soviet relations. At this conference, for the first time, the Chinese presented themselves as representatives of a great Communist power with a strong voice in policy-making for the movement as a whole. Communist China had 'arrived'. But the very moment of arrival, so long aspired to, turned out to be, ironically, also the moment of departure. Within a very few months the two great powers which had shared the honours of the Moscow Conference, which had drafted in concert the famous Moscow Declaration to be presented to the fraternal colleagues for their approval and their endorsement, were at loggerheads. And so they were to remain.

November 1957 was a great moment for the Chinese. The occasion was the fortieth anniversary of Lenin's revolution. All the chieftains of the international Communist movement had come together in Moscow to assist at the celebrations, among them Mao Tse-tung. Among them, also, a little aloof, was Kardelj, the Prime Minister of Yugoslavia. But not Tito. Khrushchev had hoped that Tito would attend, had hoped that he might be flattered into signing the Declaration which, had he done so, would have brought Yugoslavia back into the Moscow fold. But only a few weeks before Tito had been very deeply offended by the cynical manner in which Khrushchev had used him as a convenience in getting rid of Marshal Zhukov – Zhukov had been sent off on an official visit to Belgrade so that he would be out of the way while Khrushchev arranged his dismissal: he returned to Moscow fresh from his Belgrade welcome as Moscow's accredited representative to find himself in disgrace. Tito was not pleased.

The whole conference, indeed, was a characteristic example of Khrushchev's short-term manoeuvring. Moscow was full of delegations from non-Communist countries; but most of these had not the faintest idea that a grand conference was to be staged immediately after the Lenin celebrations. Then they were sent off to look at factories and collective farms while the delegates from the bloc countries stayed behind in Moscow and were briefed by the Russians and shown the Soviet draft of the Declaration, which had already been approved by the Chinese.

The Chinese were, indeed, indispensable to Khrushchev. They had already worked their passage by their behaviour over Poland and Hungary just a year before. The Polish Communist Party was led by the man, Gomulka, who had personally defied Khrushchev and, because of this, won the confidence of the anti-Communist Poles as a whole. He knew how much he owed to the Chinese for their backing in his stand. A great deal of water had flowed beneath the bridges of the Vistula since the stirring events of November 1956. The Poles were very sure of themselves and were behaving in a way quite astonishing in a nominally Communist country. Gomulka, who was as good a Communist as any man, and more fanatical than most, owed his position to his ability to secure for Poland a certain freedom from Soviet interference. He went to Moscow in November 1957 determined not to sign any document which acknowledged Soviet overlordship of the Polish Communist Party or which might suggest any sort of retrogression from the greater latitude permitted to fraternal Parties. He imagined that the Chinese would be behind him in this, and when he was faced with the draft Declaration which marked a return to an altogether harsher, more militant, more doctrinaire attitude on the part of Moscow than he had expected he set to work to persuade not only the Chinese, but also Kardelj for the Yugoslavs and Kadar for the Hungarians to modify the draft before it was submitted to the Conference. His disappointment was bitter indeed when he found that Mao Tse-tung, glorying in his new position vis-à-vis the Russians, was prepared to go along with Khrushchev.

The Declaration itself was put before the Conference on 14 November, but the non-bloc Parties had no say in it. These were busy during the first two days working out a Communist peace manifesto, which was to be published simultaneously with the Declaration. All they were required to do was to approve the Declaration without debate. And this they did, all except the Yugoslavs. As a statement of high Communist policy the Declaration was altogether more severe and belligerent in tone than Khrushchev's own report to the 20th Party Congress in Moscow two years earlier. This was not surprising. After the Polish and Hungarian revolts and the simultaneous alarm over Suez, Moscow had hardened its attitude and was in a mood to impose greater discipline. Khrushchev had all but fallen as a result of the consequences of the de-Stalinization; he had nearly had a civil war in Poland; he had had to use armed force or lose Hungary; he had seen the whole Communist world badly shaken (it will be remembered that there were many defections in 1956 and that many individual parties had been split to the point of serious injury); he had seen imperialism momentarily, if in-effectually, show its teeth at Suez. All this, together with the run-away revolt of the Soviet intellectuals in the winter of 1956–7 – there had been trouble among the workers in some of the great industrial centres too – must have made it seem urgently desirable to him to assume an air of firmness. It was a perfectly natural reaction.

There was no sharp departure from the theses of the 20th Party Congress; indeed, such a departure would have meant the reversal of Khrushchev's policies. But there was a tightening up of loose phrases and a significant shift of emphasis. It was still maintained that war was not 'fatally inevitable'; but there were no encouraging references, as there had been at the 20th Party Congress, to the 'sobering up' of unnamed Western leaders. It was still maintained that in certain cases Communism might be achieved by peaceful means, but this mode of procedure was now limited to countries which had reached an advanced state of capitalism: by implication, it was expected that Communists of the undeveloped countries in Asia, Africa, and Latin America would be compelled to use violence. Heavy stress was laid on the dynamic of national liberation movements among the remaining colonial countries and the many more lands dominated economically by the West. In general, the attitude expressed towards the imperialists was intransigeant and aggressive in the extreme: nothing could be expected of them and no quarter could be given. Finally, but by no means least, the Declaration called stridently for renewed vigilance within the Communist movement in the fight against 'dogmatism' and 'revisionism'. Both were stigmatized as evils of the worst kind, but, said the Declaration, in the conditions then obtaining, revisionism was the greater and more immediate danger of the two. The thesis of 'different roads to Socialism' still stood, but was played down. In a word, the Moscow Declaration of 1957 was a fighting and uncompromising statement of militant Communist intentions and of the necessity for strict discipline within the Communist world. Khrushchev's three pragmatical theses of the 20th Party Congress (non-inevitability of war; revolution without violence; different roads to Socialism) remained, but they had been heavily qualified. The Declaration was above all a declaration of ideological warfare on the non-Communist world in which Khrushchev's theses were not so much central, as they had been at the 20th Party Congress, but rather qualifying clauses. The Chinese, it is important to remember, not only signed this Declaration, they acted with the Russians as co-sponsors of it.[1]

2

It is time to consider the rather idiotic labels, 'dogmatism' and 'revisionism'. We shall be living with them for the rest of this narrative, and from now on I do not propose to enclose them in inverted commas. They are key-words in the Communist vocabulary; and although I shall avoid cant words wherever possible, dogmatism and revisionism are inescapable. There are no other words to use as synonyms; fundamentalism and experimentalism will not quite do.

They were first used by Lenin. They are part of the not very rich vocabulary of Leninist anathema – Left Deviationist, Right

Deviationist, Left Opportunist, Right Opportunist, Fractionalist, and a few others.

Lenin was Lenin. He was right and everybody else was wrong unless they agreed with him in detail. Disagreement was vicious. The capitalists were naturally wrong: it was their historical duty to be wrong. But self-styled Socialists should be right. In simple, human terms Lenin understood by dogmatists all those revolutionary colleagues who tried to check his experimental flights, his free adaptations of Marx and Engels, by quoting at him texts from Marx and Engels; by revisionists he understood all those who essayed their own experimental flights, their own adaptations of Marx and Engels. The first important revisionists were Bernstein and Kautsky, two leading Marxists who at the turn of the century advanced the argument that social revolution might best be brought about by 'evolutionary' (perhaps parliamentary) means, as opposed to violent revolution. These unfortunates did not live to see their theories confirmed, as they are in the process of being confirmed in various western European countries today. They were pursued for the rest of their lives by Lenin with a scorn and fury and a display of invective modelled directly on the manners and prose style of Karl Marx.

Dogmatism was a later phenomenon. It did not manifest itself until the Bolsheviks, under pressure from the facts of life, began behaving in an un-Marxist way and adapting or distorting Marx's texts to rationalize and justify their conduct. As time went on dogmatism came to mean failure to recognize changing realities, the parroting of Leninist texts learnt by heart, regardless of their present relevance, and in a manner 'calculated to alienate the Party from the masses'. Revisionism, on the other hand, as defined in the 1957 Moscow Declaration, covered all reforming movements within the Party which denied 'the historical necessity of the proletarian revolution' and which offended against 'Leninist principles for the construction of the Party'.

Under Stalin, 'dogmatist' was a charge hurled indiscriminately at all those who raised their eyebrows at Stalin's sudden opportunist switches of policy – for example his destruction of the German Communist Party in the 1930s, his wooing of the Nazis in 1939; 'revisionist' was the smear word for all those who objected to police-rule. As the Sino–Soviet dispute gathered way, neither side wished to burn its bridges by attacking the other openly and unequivocally for all the world to see; each side chose a symbolic object to represent the other. Thus Mao constructed a model of Khrushchev, christened it Tito, stuck pins in it, and cursed it as the arch-revisionist; Khrushchev chose Hoxha of Albania as the name for his model of Mao Tse-tung, and cursed it as the arch-dogmatist. The fact that this schoolroom behaviour made the majesty of Moscow and Pekin look absurd evidently troubled neither side in the least: Communists, no matter what other short-comings they may suffer, have never worried about looking ridiculous.

Thus when, in 1962, the Chinese, attacking Khrushchev's policies in their press, but still not mentioning Khrushchev or the Soviet Union by name, began making thoughtful comparisons between these and the heresies of Bernstein and Kautsky, it was the hoisting of a storm-signal. And, as we shall see, when in March 1963 *Red Flag*, the Chinese Party fortnightly, announced that the present dispute was the third great dispute in the history of practical Marxism it was a formal declaration of a fight to the finish. The first great dispute cited by Pekin was the dispute between Lenin on the one hand and, on the other, Kautsky, Bernstein, and 'other right-wing opportunists'; the second was the dispute between Stalin on the one hand and Trotsky and Bukharin on the other. Lenin had conquered, and so had Stalin. The third was the dispute between the 'genuine Marxist', Mao Tse-tung, on the one hand and the revisionist Khrushchev, and all his contemptible allies, on the other.[2]

3

In Moscow in November 1957 there was not a breath of this. Khrushchev and Mao acted in accord, and if anything it was Mao at that time who was still inclined to be more revisionist than Khrushchev. The only disagreement took place at a lower level when Gomulka of Poland and Togliatti of Italy made common ground in their insistence that dogmatism, not revisionism, was the most immediate danger – and, of course, the Yugoslavs passionately believed the same. But at that time neither Gomulka nor Togliatti was thinking specifically of the

Chinese when they attacked the dogmatists. They were thinking of the Russians, who with Chinese support were reasserting their rigid central control over the activities of all fraternal parties and at the same time, by the wording of the Declaration, threatening Italian dreams of 'poly-centrism', much to the delight of the French delegation, and Polish dreams of developing the Polish way.

Indeed, the most remarkable aspect of this hastily prepared conference was the apparent lack of awareness on the part of any of the participants, the Russians and the Chinese included, of what was really happening inside the world-Communist movement, of the various forces that were crystallizing out in contradictory directions even as the Declaration appeared to be stabilizing the situation, and of the logical consequences of certain lines of thought and behaviour already implicit in the recent conduct of Moscow and Pekin. It was, looking back, as though Khrushchev was so intent on the immediate task of reasserting his own authority over a movement threatened with widespread fission, and as though Mao Tse-tung was so pleased at having at last been recognized by the Russians as the head of a great Communist power, that neither had a moment's thought to spare to consider his future practical policy in detail. This was a failure which was to cost the Chinese dear.

It was, indeed, such an obvious failure on the part of both Khrushchev and Mao that one is tempted to discount it and to conclude that since they must have perceived the latent differences piling up between them the Moscow Declaration amounted to a conscious papering over of the cracks. But this was not so. Each side read into the Declaration what it wanted to read; and it is fairly easy to see why and how. They were contemplating it from widely separated standpoints, and each was unaware of where the other stood.

To simplify exceedingly, the basic difference arose from the fact that Khrushchev viewed the Declaration as an instrument of Soviet State policy, while Mao viewed it as an instrument of the revolutionary process. Nobody was more anxious than Khrushchev to restore order to the Communist movement, to impose discipline upon it, and to present to the outer world a tough united front. In this he was perfectly in accord with Mao.

Where the two men were not at all in accord was in their motives. Khrushchev's Leninist reaffirmation had as its main purpose the strengthening of Soviet State power, the re-establishment of Soviet control (now in convenient alliance with China) over the Communist world, above all the European satellites, so that he could continue undisturbed with his long-term plans to reach some sort of an accommodation with the West, with the United States in particular, while building up at home the strength and prosperity of the Soviet Union. Revolutionary considerations were only secondary to this. But with Mao it was quite otherwise. For him the restatement of militant revolutionary doctrine was not a political expedient; it was quite simply a call to action. For him the drive towards world revolution was the very justification of the Communist position; whereas for Khrushchev, vaguely enough, the revolutionary appeal and the revolutionary threat were cards in the hand of the Soviet Union as a power.

This is to over-simplify, if only because China too was beginning to think and feel as a power, while Khrushchev, on his side, was, and is, clearly influenced in his attitude to the world by his Leninist inheritance. But the opposition was strong enough: China existed for the revolution; the revolution existed for Russia. And although both Khrushchev and Mao must have been aware of this with half their minds the logic of the situation escaped them in the excitement of the moment. They failed to connect.

The remarkable thing was that China was already preparing to go her own way. A very serious aftermath of the 1956 explosions among the European satellites had been the realization in Moscow of a new fact: in order to restore some sort of stability to its East European empire it was urgently necessary for the Soviet Union to reverse a trend which had been in operation for the past decade. Instead of plundering the satellites in the interests of the Soviet Union, Khrushchev had now to put something back. He had to put a good deal back – in all, in 1957, something like a billion dollars. One of the immediate consequences of this unforeseen expenditure, and by far the most important, was that others had to go short. And the chief sufferers were the Chinese. Pekin was very hard hit by this diversion of funds; but it also had its advantages, at least in the eyes of some of the Chinese leaders. China would have to rely more on her own unaided efforts and, as a result, could aspire to more complete independence. As early as May 1957, Li Fu-chun, the Chairman of the State Planning Commission, had warned the Chinese that they must rely on their own strength 'as much as possible',[3] and a month later the Chairman of the State Economic Commission, Po Yi-po, said much the same thing: China must reduce her 'reliance on foreign countries'.[4]

These warnings, coming at a time when the Chinese economy was running into serious difficulties, boded ill. They also, one would have thought, struck an ominous note for Moscow: allies who suddenly decide that their future depends on 'going it alone' are apt to become unreliable partners and, making a virtue of necessity, develop a mood of overweening brashness. No thought of this appears to have passed through Khrushchev's mind at the time of the Moscow Conference; but within a matter of months precisely this was to happen, and even while Mao was performing in Moscow as the bland and benevolent, if stern, elder statesman of the Communist world, there must have been individuals, or groups, within the Party leadership in Pekin who were already consciously heading for the great swing to the Left which was to manifest itself first in the establishment of the communes, in the Great Leap Forward; then in a mood of anti-Soviet chauvinism.

Something else had happened shortly before the Moscow Conference which, more than anything, was to accelerate the development of the latent differences between Khrushchev and Mao.

In August 1957 Moscow announced to a somewhat sceptical but more than slightly apprehensive world that the Soviet Union had conducted a successful test of an 'inter-continental, multi-stage ballistic rocket'. Very few people knew much about multi-stage rockets in those days. They were soon to know more. On 4 October the first *sputnik* was launched, trailing clouds of Russian glory as it bleeped its way through space. On 3 November, on the eve of the 40th anniversary of the Revolution, the performance was repeated. The Russians were triumphant, the Americans were cast into the lower depths of gloom. The Chinese, who had nothing whatsoever to do with the affair, went off their heads with joy: a Communist country, the Soviet Union, had utterly outstripped the imperialists in the development of weaponry; now was the time to exert the power of the Socialist camp and put unremitting pressure on the West in the interests of world revolution.

Khrushchev, while freely boasting in terms appropriate to the mood of vulgarity which had overcome both camps – a depressing echo of pre-1914, which demonstrated that vainglorious ostentation was not a monopoly of a decadent upper class – was not so sure. While the Chinese press insisted on the positive aspects of the new superiority of Soviet arms, Khrushchev preferred to dwell on its negative aspects. While the Chinese expected the trumpets to sound and the walls of Jericho to fall, Khrushchev preferred to talk about the deterrent value of his new and unholy toys.

But the difference in the Soviet and the Chinese assessment of the impact of the *sputniks* seemed to escape both Khrushchev and Mao. In his speech to the Conference Mao injected into the debate two phrases which were to become famous and symbolic of Sino–Soviet differences, although, at the time, they appeared to be nothing more than a picturesquely personal way of expressing a viewpoint held jointly by the Russians and the Chinese. The first was his remark about the East wind prevailing over the West wind; the second was the image of the 'paper tiger' as a term of contempt for the imperialists – although, as he said, he had first used this image in his conversation with Anna Louise Strong in 1946, referring to Chiang Kai-shek's forces, which had a terrifying aspect, which greatly outnumbered the Communist forces, but which were doomed to defeat.[5]

On the face of it there would appear to be very little difference between Mao's contemptuous reference to imperialism as a paper tiger and Khrushchev's own brashly confident phrase 'We shall bury you!'. The same could be said of Mao's image of the East wind prevailing over the West wind and Khrushchev's insistence that the balance of power between Socialism and imperialism had shifted in favour of Socialism. Certainly no significant difference was perceived by Western observers; almost certainly no such difference was perceived by Khrushchev or Mao. But the difference was there all the same, and, as I have said, it stemmed from the basic attitudes of the two men. When Mao, pursuing his image of the winds, said in his speech to the Moscow Conference: 'I am of the opinion that the international situation has reached a new turning-point. . . . That is to say, the Socialist forces are overwhelmingly superior to the imperialist forces' – when he said this it meant more than a rather ebullient version of Khrushchev's expressed confidence in the capacity of the Socialist camp to hold its own in face of imperialism, to avert a catastrophic war, and in the end to conquer without war: it was an implied call to action. What was the point of being over-whelmingly superior unless you brought that superiority im-mediately to bear?

What seems to have happened is that Khrushchev and Mao at Moscow took their own attitudes so much for granted that each assumed his attitude was shared by the other. In the immediate years to come there was to be fearful recrimination over the famous Declaration, jointly sponsored by Khrushchev and Mao. Each was to accuse the other of departing from the line laid down in it. Here the Chinese were at fault. They had endorsed both the 20th Party Congress Resolutions and the Moscow Declara-tion, almost certainly without grasping the full implications of what they were doing. Where the Chinese were in the right later on was in their grave accusation that Khrushchev had departed from Leninism. But they would have been in a much stronger position if they had protested first in 1956 at the 20th Party Congress, then in 1957 at the Moscow Conference. They were much too slow off the mark – almost certainly because they themselves had not thought their position as a great Communist power in the modern world right through.

There was a key passage in Mao's Moscow speech which was much later to assume tremendous importance in the conflict as it developed, above all in the defence of the Chinese position as stated in the crucial series of newspaper articles which started with 'The Differences between Signor Togliatti and Us' in the *People's Daily* of 31 December 1962:

In our struggle with the enemy we formed over a long period the concept that strategically we should treat our enemies with contempt but that tactically we should take them seriously. That is to say, we should treat the enemy with contempt in general and yet, at the same time, take him seriously in regard to each and every concrete problem. If we do not treat the enemy as a whole with contempt we shall be committing the error of opportunism. . . . But in dealing with concrete problems and particular enemies, if we do not take them seriously we shall be committing the error of adventurism.

This formulation, in years to come, was to appear prophetic. It seemed ready-made to suit the Chinese view of Khrushchev's behaviour in Cuba, and was used to characterize it. He had committed the sin of opportunism by laying too much stress on the strength of imperialism as a whole. He had then committed the sin of adventurism by not taking the immediate difficulties in the way of his Cuban action seriously enough. He was then to commit a new sin, 'capitulationism', in retreating in face of American pressure.

At the time it appeared to be no more than a conventional essay in doctrinal exegesis, and so it was intended. The catch, the latent difference between China and Russia, lay in divergencies of interpretation. And the Chinese were soon to show that their own appreciation of the possible differed from Khrushchev's. They began, a month after the Conference, in an article in *World Culture* for 20 December 1957:

The absolute superiority of the Soviet Union in inter-continental ballistic missiles has placed the striking capabilities of the United States in an inferior position. . . . The Soviet inter-continental ballistic missiles can not only reach any military base in Central Europe, Asia, or Africa, but they can also force the United States, for the first time in history, into a position from which neither escape nor the power to strike back is possible.

Soon, in the matter of the Middle East crisis in the summer of 1958, the Chinese, urging the Russians to use their superiority to halt the Western landings in Lebanon and Jordan, showed the sort of thing they had in mind.

Chapter Eight

CHINA SWINGS LEFT

I

THE seeds of difference were germinating at the end of 1957, but they had not yet sprouted. Mao Tse-tung could regard the outcome of the Moscow Conference with considerable satisfaction. His influence on Soviet policy stood higher than ever before, and it was to persist into the summer of 1958. At the Conference itself he could take credit for restoring the united Communist front. He had followed up his positive action in the Hungarian and Polish crises of 1956 by presiding over Gomulka's submission to Moscow. He had helped to check the wild movement towards poly-centrism. He had joined with Khrushchev in introducing important reservations into the new doctrine of war and peace and violent revolution and in putting a much sharper emphasis on the importance of national liberation movements. He must have believed (who did not?) that Khrushchev would shortly be exploiting to the full his spectacular-seeming lead in space. It was a pity about Yugoslavia. The conference would have been very nicely rounded off if Tito had signed the Declaration; but by refusing to do so he had shown his true colours and must be made to pay: there were far too many European Communists, above all Gomulka within the bloc and Togliatti outside it, who would exploit to the full in their own national interests any tenderness towards the Yugoslavs. Finally, while demonstratively insisting that the Soviet Union must be accepted as the formal leader of the Socialist camp, Mao had reached the position (what more could he ask?) at which he alone among world Communist leaders had been invited by Moscow to cooperate in laying down the law to the lesser Parties: all Communist Parties were equal, of course, but the Soviet Party had always been more equal than the others; now the Chinese Party was more equal too.

But at this very moment events were in train which were to bring out the latent differences between China and the Soviet

Union. As so often in the Communist world these events had their roots in domestic politics.

Pekin was embarking on a course which was to involve a tremendous swing from the right to the left, to carry them far from the mild, experimental mood implicit in the Bandung principles of 1955. Very soon it was to lead to the adoption of the harshest and most uncompromising attitude towards the whole of the outside world, and to split the movement. A combination of internal and external circumstances was beginning to justify all those voices, muffled hitherto, which called for the strongest assertion either of Chinese nationalism, or Leninist principles, or both, regardless of the immediate cost in suffering. In Moscow this trend was not seen for what it was by either Khrushchev or Mao himself: it was masked by the accidental fact that Khrushchev, after the 1956 explosions, was compelled to adopt a more harsh and uncompromising line. But for Khrushchev this was no more than a tactical necessity: once he had steadied the boat he was to go forward again with his old policies – on and on to the Summit. For Mao the change was much more than tactical. It was a genuine change of course.

Perhaps the first internal cause was the failure of Mao's brief summer of the Hundred Flowers. There seems every reason to suppose that when in the early summer of 1957, under the slogan 'Let a Hundred Flowers Bloom', Mao had relaxed his hold on the reins, he had genuinely believed that the reconstruction of China in the Communist image had been so successful that he could afford to give his people their heads, and that he was altogether horrified and shocked by the flood of criticism, the violent spirit of rejection, which suddenly welled up. At any rate, within a matter of weeks the Hundred Flowers had bloomed and perished, and stern discipline was restored.

At the same time, the economic situation in China was very ugly indeed. Rationing was stringent. Factories, railways, shipping, were being brought to a standstill for lack of coal. There had been severe natural calamities and, in addition, collectivized agriculture was failing to produce enough food. There were those who in face of these hard facts wanted to retreat temporarily, to adopt a slower tempo while the economy was steadily consolidated – much the same sort of solution that Lenin had sought with his New Economic Policy in 1922. There were others who wanted to push on, faster and yet faster, rather than risk running the economy into a deep bog. And at precisely this time, as we have seen, the Soviet Union turned out to be a broken reed. There may have been hidden reasons for its failure to come forward with more aid; but the billion-dollar advance to the European satellites certainly had a decisive effect. China was increasingly in a mood to go it alone, and damn the consequences. She was already aware of Soviet reluctance to let her have atomic weapons. And the debates at the Moscow Conference, which ended in the compromise Declaration, must also have shown her that Khrushchev as a revolutionary leader was not really to be trusted.

Something of all this was indicated by the Chinese Prime Minister, Liu Shao-chi, who, speaking at the Chinese Party Congress in May 1958, admitted that there had been deep conflict. But this, he then indicated, had been resolved. Liu made it quite clear that the radicals had won. He violently attacked the go-slowers (who, it is generally believed, included the Prime Minister, Chou En-lai), and declared that the sole preoccupation of the Party was 'to build our country, in the shortest possible time, into a great Socialist country'. It was in this mood that the communes and the policy of the Great Leap Forward were born.[1]

2

Khrushchev, meanwhile, proceeded cautiously. One aspect of China's determination to go it alone was that it allowed Pekin to put pressure on Moscow without fear of crippling economic reprisals. Pressure was applied in the international sphere in two distinct ways. First, in May, the Chinese Communist Party formulated its line in the matter of Yugoslavia, from which it was never again to budge, and it was set out in a resolution of the Chinese Party Congress dated 25 May:

In a wild attempt to undermine and disintegrate the Communist Parties of various countries they [the Yugoslavs] have propagated a series of fallacious theories. They deny the leading role of the Communist Party in Socialist revolution and Socialist construction; they attack the Communist and Workers' Parties in the Socialist countries, and slander the Communist Parties in the capitalist countries. . . . This thoroughly revisionist programme is put forward for the purpose of splitting the international Communist movement.

For good measure, the resolution went on to charge the Yugoslavs with 'playing the inglorious role of provocateurs and interventionists in the counter-revolutionary uprising in Hungary'.

This was much further than Khrushchev could conceivably have wanted to go, unless he was on the point of reversing his whole line of policy. Certainly he was angry with the Yugoslavs. Certainly he could blame them for encouraging rebellious elements in Poland, Hungary, and elsewhere. Certainly he was irritated by their refusal to sign the Moscow declaration and by the resolutions passed by the Yugoslav Congress in Ljubliana early in 1958, which he had himself boycotted. But he had said nothing to suggest that he was on the point of turning his back on all hope of the ultimate reconciliation with Marshal Tito, which he had done so much to achieve. And very soon it became apparent that he had no intention at all of abandoning his general line of policy, above all his *rapprochement* with the West, which had been interrupted only by Hungary and Suez.

But what was he to do, faced with this unequivocal Chinese initiative? If he went on with his wooing of Tito it would make it clear to all the world that he was already, in the spring of 1958, in conflict with China. And he needed China's backing in his renewed attempt to achieve a Summit meeting with the American President. Yugoslavia would have to wait. And so, with almost precipitate haste, Khrushchev publicly endorsed the Chinese condemnation, and, at Sofia, himself accused Tito of acting like 'a Trojan horse for the imperialists'. Far more to the point, from the Chinese point of view, he withheld the economic aid already promised to Yugoslavia. Finally, a month later, obviously still seeking to please the Chinese (though this has so far never been said), he presided over the judicial murder of Imre Nagy, who had been under Yugoslav protection when he was snatched away by Soviet police.

The next thing that happened was that the campaign for a

Summit meeting was suddenly brought to a halt just as Khrushchev flew off to Pekin to talk to Mao in August.

3

Here is the occasion for a word about Chinese pressure on Khrushchev. During 1958, and even long afterwards, it was quite a common thing for Western observers to question the very existence of any such pressure. How, conceivably, they asked, could a country as backward as China, standing in so much need of Russian material help, exercise pressure on the Soviet leadership? And what evidence was there that Khrushchev had to face criticism at home from supporters of the Chinese position?

A little later in this narrative, when we come to examine in detail what happened at Bucarest and in Moscow in 1960, we shall see precisely what pressure the Chinese were able to bring. And it was a formidable pressure. It was not a matter of Mao saying to Khrushchev in so many words: if you don't denounce Tito and stop giving him aid we shall overthrow you. The sort of pressure he brought to bear was much more insidious. If, the argument almost certainly ran, you persist in certain policies which we consider to be anti-Marxist and anti-Leninist we shall not be able to subscribe to them. Indeed, we shall expose them for what they are to the view of all the fraternal Parties and ask them to choose between us. You may win the first round. Your strength is much greater than ours. But your authority will be very badly shaken; you, not we (because it is you who are deviating from the proper path), will have on your conscience the destruction of Communist unity. And, in the long run, because we are right and in due course will be seen to be right, we shall win. Nor is it only a matter of the smaller Parties: there are plenty of men in the Soviet Union, known to us, who sympathize with our view, and many more who will pretend to sympathize with it in order to put you down.

I am not suggesting that Mao ever said this to Khrushchev in so many words in 1958 (he certainly did, through his spokesmen, in 1960). But this sort of threat must have been implicit in all his dealings. He had saved the Soviet empire in Europe in Novem-

ber 1956. He had forced the Poles to accept the suzerainty of
Moscow in November 1957. At that confused time, when
Khrushchev had only just succeeded in asserting himself above
all his rivals, Communists all over the world felt a greater
respect for the massive, stern, but seemingly noble image of
Mao Tse-tung, raised high above intrigue, than for this new
saviour in Moscow who was always getting into trouble and
behaving sometimes more like a drunken peasant horse-dealer
than a great statesman. The Chinese provided for the Communist movement a great attractive power. Where would Khrushchev
be without them at his back?

Khrushchev had his troubles still at home. He had broken the
anti-Party group, and there was nobody left in high office to
challenge his supremacy effectively. But he was still a suspect
and distrusted figure in some exceedingly important circles. He
was dictator, but he was dictator, as it were, by consent of the
new Soviet élite, who, aware of his special genius and ability,
needed what he alone could provide. But there were limits. And
throughout the country was scattered a host of men whom he had
offended or displaced: technocrats and managers in their
thousands who had been affronted by his new industrial policy
which had broken their hold on Moscow; Party functionaries at
all levels who were outraged, sometimes by what he had done,
more often by his way of doing it; agriculturalists, industrialists,
economists, whom he had made into scapegoats for past failures; soldiers too. Malenkov had disappeared; he has never been
seen since he was sent off to his putative power-station in
Siberia. But Molotov, banished to Ulan Bator in Mongolia, was
still very much alive, still a figure very much revered by many of
the older Party men – and he was close to China. In 1958 it
would not have been at all inconceivable that a public dis-
association of China from Khrushchev's policies might end in
the fall of Khrushchev himself.

At any rate, he bowed to China's denunciation of Tito; and,
a little later, again in deference to Mao's wishes, he abandoned,
for the time being, his wooing of President Eisenhower. But only
until, in 1959, he felt strong enough to start again.

4

The crisis in the Middle East in the summer of 1958 was the first demonstration to the world, and to the Chinese, that Khrushchev meant what he said when he spoke of the imperative necessity of avoiding war. When British and American troops made their landing in Lebanon after the Iraqi revolution of 13 July this operation was seen both by the Russians and the Chinese not as a preparation for the defence of Lebanon, but as the prelude for an invasion of Iraq. Indeed, the build-up in Lebanon was so powerful that it was not only Communists who thought this. Khrushchev's reaction was not to put 'volunteers' into Iraq but to get the West to an emergency Summit meeting before it was too late. Certainly he ordered troop movements under Marshal Rokossowski, but that these were purely defensive was at once demonstrated by the note of desperation in his appeal. If war was to be averted, there must be a Summit meeting at once: 'the guns have already started to speak'. He was appalled by the dilemma with which he would be faced if the Western allies moved into Iraq: either he would have to move against them, with the fearful probability of running into a major nuclear war, or he would have to let the Iraqi liberation movement be destroyed, without moving a finger. Stalin was strong enough to permit himself the luxury of betraying his protégés: he needed no prestige to bolster him up. Khrushchev was vulnerable all along the line.

Since the allies had no intention of attacking in Iraq, the crisis collapsed of its own accord. But not before it had taught the West, and the Chinese, a lesson. The Western world was encouraged by that lesson. The Chinese were not. What is more, they showed their disapproval of Khrushchev's timidity. They conspicuously failed to join in the appeal for a summit meeting. And the *People's Daily* took an altogether tougher line than Khrushchev. In an editorial which appeared on 19 July, the day after Khrushchev's appeal, entitled 'The Countries and Peoples of the World Who Love Peace and Freedom Cannot Look On with Folded Arms', came the passage:

'Nothing can be saved by yielding to evil, and coddling wrong only helps the devil.' The histories of the aggressive wars launched by Hitler Germany and Japan are still fresh in the memory of the whole world and are sufficient to bring this lesson home. Consequently, if the U.S.–British aggressors refuse to withdraw from Lebanon and Jordan, and insist on expanding their aggression, then the only course left to the people of the world is to hit the aggressors on the head! . . . The imperialists have always bullied the weak and been afraid of the strong. The only language they understand is that of force.

This was not Khrushchev's line at all. In his letter of the day before addressed to President Eisenhower he said:

We address you not from a position of intimidation but from a position of reason. We believe at this momentous hour that it would be more reasonable not to bring the heated atmosphere to boiling point; it is sufficiently inflammable as it is.

When he wrote this he was already aware of what the Chinese *People's Daily* had said two days before: 'There cannot be the slightest indulgence towards American imperialism's act of aggression. . . . Therefore let the people of the whole world take emergency action.' Six days after the letter to Eisenhower, the *Liberation Army Daily* was boasting that the Socialist camp did not fear war because 'the balance of power in our favour has never been so great.' This was written some days after Pekin had at last endorsed Khrushchev's appeal for a Summit, no doubt because Khrushchev had made it plain that he would not fight so long as the West kept out of Iraq. On 23 July Khrushchev accepted, on conditions, Eisenhower's counter-proposal for a Summit within the framework of the Security Council. But five days later he withdrew his acceptance, on the grounds that what he had agreed to was a 'special five-power meeting, not a regular session of the Security Council'. Whether he did this under pressure from Pekin or not we do not know, or whether he judged that the crisis was over. What we do know is that the expressed line of Pekin and the actual conduct of Khrushchev were identical with, though a good deal less spectacular than, the expressed line of Pekin and the actual conduct of Khrushchev just over four years later. Then Khrushchev, again appealing to reason and the spirit of moderation, withdrew his rockets from Cuba and was accused by China of echoing Munich. From the summer of 1958 there was no more real ambiguity in Sino–Soviet relations. We can plot them with certainty from now on.

Chapter Nine

KHRUSHCHEV UNDER FIRE

I

IN 1959 Khrushchev began to take the offensive. In February of that year he convened a Party Congress in Moscow which had a number of purposes. The most obvious was to celebrate his victory over the Anti-Party Group and underline the fact that a new chapter of the post-Stalin era had opened. But a subsidiary object was to find a face-saving formula about the timing of the millennium in different lands. All Socialist countries would achieve Communism 'more or less at the same time' was the new approach. He left it to the exegesists to discuss how much difference there was between 'more' and 'less', and this they settled down happily to do when the Congress was over.

Also in February Khrushchev received Mr Macmillan. By working up a rather acute scare over Berlin he had convinced the British Prime Minister, and many more besides, that a Summit meeting was highly desirable in the interests of peace (almost certainly the Berlin affair had been manufactured especially for that purpose). He was able to seize the opportunity to be rude to Mr Macmillan, which showed the world that he was really a leading international statesman, and to prepare the way for the visit of Mr Nixon, which itself paved the way for his own visit to the United States.

He did more. In May on a visit to Enver Hoxha in Albania he met the then Chinese Minister of Defence, Marshal Peng Teh-huai. Marshal Peng was bitterly opposed to the Great Leap Forward and the communes, and he had, as a member of the Chinese Politburo, prepared an elaborate memorandum setting forth his views. In Tirana he took the opportunity of showing this memorandum to Khrushchev, before presenting it to his colleagues at home.[1] Shortly after he had put it before his own colleagues Marshal Peng was arrested in the great purge of 'right-wing opportunists', degraded, and sentenced to a period of intensive 'reindoctrination' in the most humble circumstances

(Khrushchev was later to taunt the Chinese with having sent Peng 'to a Labour camp' for daring to talk with his fraternal comrades.[2]) It is still not clear whether the Chinese colleagues knew of Peng's 'treachery' before his arrest, or whether it did not come out until he was under duress. It does not matter. The fact that the Chinese Defence Minister was openly opposed to the communes and to the whole of Chinese domestic and strategic policy at that time, and that he felt about it strongly enough to sue for Khrushchev's support in face of his own colleagues, was the sign of a very deep cleavage in the government of China. At the very least it must have encouraged Khrushchev to pursue his own way.

In August of that year the Chinese crossed the Indian border, and the Soviet Union assumed a conspicuously neutral attitude, although much earlier the invasion of Tibet had been vociferously applauded.

In September Khrushchev at last achieved his visit to America.

It is impossible to exaggerate the climacteric importance of this event in Khrushchev's eyes. Time and time again he had angled for the invitation, laying himself open to snubs of a kind which no other statesman in the world would have dared to risk. But from his point of view it was worth it. When President Eisenhower's invitation at last came, it established the Soviet Union for all the world to see as the acknowledged equal of the United States of America; it established Khrushchev personally at home as the man who could work miracles; it gave him the chance of presenting himself to the world as the one man who could save the peace. The Moscow press was beside itself with exultation. It spoke almost recklessly of the coming visit as marking an historical 'turning point' and the beginning of a new age. Was this a direct retort to Mao's idea of a turning-point, as expressed at the Moscow Conference in 1957?

How far Khrushchev had committed himself to achieving this apotheosis, the formal visit of the head of a great Communist power to the head of a great capitalist power, was never fully appreciated in the West. Overawed, as we so often are, by the immense power of the Soviet Union, its sheer size as well as the brilliance of its warlike techniques, it is very hard for us to realize the sense of insecurity vis-à-vis the outside world which haunts the ordinary Russian, who has suffered so much at the hands of the invader. It is an insecurity which stems from various causes: consciousness of backwardness in many ways, knowledge of the fearful destruction inflicted in past wars by far smaller powers, the sense of being ostracized by the West. And this feeling of insecurity was deliberately fostered by Stalin for decades, by Khrushchev too, on occasion – the object being to stress the standing threat from the capitalist powers, in order to divert attention from evils nearer home and to justify the emphasis on heavy industry and the absence of so many material amenities. Khrushchev wished, at least for the time being, to present himself as the man who could bring real security to the Soviet people by averting the standing threat from the West.

In the summer of 1959 he had made an extremely interesting remark to a group of American State Governors who were then touring the Soviet Union. When he repeated the sense of this remark for the benefit of the Soviet people in a speech at Dnepropetrovsk on 28 July his remark was elevated from a calculated indiscretion into an act of policy. At Dnepropetrovsk he said:

'Our country and the United States are the two most mighty Powers in the world. If other countries fight among themselves they can be separated; but if war breaks out between America and our country, no one will be able to stop it. It will be a catastrophe on a colossal scale.'

It is possible to view this remark as so much camouflage. Many would so view it. Khrushchev, they would say, was deliberately seeking to lull the West into a false sense of security by playing down ideological differences and the drive to global Communism and pretending that the Soviet Union was a power like any other power – though greater than all but one – with whom reasonable accommodations might be reached. I do not believe this. I believe, on the contrary, that Khrushchev was here pursuing a genuine line of thought, not his only line of thought (it is a privilege of statesmen, as of the rest of us, to run alternative lines of thought simultaneously, sometimes self-contradictory), but genuine all the same. Certainly the Chinese took him at his word. Very soon now we shall see them accusing

Khrushchev of selling China, and the world revolution too, down the river in order to reach a Soviet–American accord.

'Our country ...' Here is Khrushchev speaking not at all as head of the world Communist movement, but as the chief of state of a great secular power. 'If other countries fight among themselves they can be separated ...' China has no nuclear arms ... If China fights India, if she fights anywhere at all, the fight can be broken up. The Socialist camp is forgotten: all that matters is some sort of working co-existence between the Soviet Union and the United States; between them they can police the world.

Two months later Khrushchev was deep in confabulation with President Eisenhower, the other chief policeman. The story is familiar. Khrushchev flew back to Moscow exuding the 'spirit of Camp David'. The American President, he said, had shown himself to be a wise and statesmanlike figure, a man of peace who could be relied upon to keep the professional war-mongers of the Pentagon well under control. A new dawn was breaking.

Almost at once Khrushchev flew off to Pekin. The occasion was the tenth anniversary of the Chinese revolution. It was the very moment for an imposing show of solidarity: to fail at such a time to emphasize the inviolable unity of the Socialist camp in general and Sino–Soviet brotherhood in particular could only mean the existence of a rift deeper than anyone had until then suspected. In fact, failure was complete. And it was this visit of Khrushchev's to Pekin in October 1959 that brought final confirmation of the existence of a major quarrel. Until then it had been obvious that there were differences, sometimes acute. But these differences appeared to be quite manageable, and they were not apparent to the world at large; only the close student of Communist affairs could deduce in outline what they were about. October 1959 was, thus, a critical turning point in yet another sense: for the first time both Khrushchev and Mao showed themselves ready to advertise the differences between them to the Communist world as a whole and to attentive outsiders.

We know now that Khrushchev's praise of President Eisenhower was received in Pekin with outraged incredulity. Over a year later the Secretary General of the Chinese Communist Party, Teng Hsiao-ping, speaking behind closed doors in Moscow at the great Conference of eighty-one Communist Parties, referred to it with such depth of feeling that it might have been uttered only the day before. We shall examine Teng's speech as a whole in a later chapter. But it is worth recording here that part of it which referred to the events of the early autumn of 1959, which was the moment at which the dispute broke its banks. On 9 September, Teng said, Tass had published a 'tendentious communiqué' about the Sino–Indian dispute. 'This communiqué revealed our differences to the world.' Almost at once the Soviet leaders had started denigrating the Chinese leaders and flattering the imperialist leaders. This reached a climax on Khrushchev's return from the United States. His behaviour then had been intolerable: 'No considerations of diplomatic protocol can explain away, or excuse, Khrushchev's tactless eulogy of Eisenhower and other imperialists, when he said in public that Eisenhower enjoyed the complete support of the American people.'[2]

It was this 'tactless eulogy' which was still ringing in Chinese ears when Khrushchev arrived in Pekin. It was not a happy visit. We do not know what was said between Khrushchev and Mao; but we know enough about the Soviet and Chinese moods at that time to guess some of it. Khrushchev's attitude towards India, towards America, towards Formosa and the off-shore islands, towards the communes and the Great Leap Forward must all have come under fire, to say nothing of the behaviour of Soviet technicians in China and Soviet intrigues against the Chinese Party – as symbolized by the affair of Marshal Peng.

Neither Mao nor any other senior Chinese leader made a speech of welcome or a speech of farewell. There was no communiqué issued after the conversations. Khrushchev himself made two public speeches in which he said many of the proper things. He did not praise Eisenhower, but he did insist that there were many encouraging signs of a much more 'realistic and sober approach' to matters of war and peace on the part of responsible imperialist leaders. He stressed the reality of his policy of co-existence, seen as an enduring policy and not simply as an act of calculated deception. Most strikingly of all, and obviously with the Indian border trouble in mind, as well as the possibility of further, larger conflicts, he came out flatly against war as an instrument of policy: force, he said, must absolutely not be used against the capitalist world, no matter how strong the Communists might be. During all this time the Chinese press went on blasting away at the unspeakable imperialists hatching war. One of the most uncompromising speeches made at this time was by the Chinese Foreign Minister, Marshal Chen Yi.[3]

Returning to Moscow after this disastrous visit, Khrushchev seized the occasion to tour parts of the Maritime Provinces and eastern Siberia, from Vladivostock to Irkutsk. He had a great deal to say, but he spoke in a more relaxed and confident mood than he had ever shown before. His Chinese visit was not mentioned. The big problems of a divided world were scarcely touched upon. Instead, Khrushchev chose this moment, when the Chinese were struggling for their very survival with natural calamities and the fearful consequences of their own mistakes, to expatiate at length and on every possible occasion on the growing prosperity of the Soviet Union. He felt sure enough of himself to make fun of the naïve dreams of the Russian people in the early days of the revolution. But he substituted dreams of his own. And the Chinese, desperately in need of more Soviet aid, marching their peasants to work in regiments in the fearful battle to increase production, could overhear him saying, one can guess with what feelings, that already at Bratsk (with its colossal power station on the Angara river) the workers were going to be put on a six-hour day. He said more: 'I am deeply convinced that the time is not far off when, on the basis of the further development of production, science, and technology . . . people will work only three or four hours a day in our country.'

'Our country' again.

Meanwhile Mao went on behaving towards India, towards America too, as though Khrushchev did not exist.

But not for long. Later in October the Soviet Party sent a circular letter to all fraternal parties explaining and justifying Khrushchev's attitude towards America. In the following month the Soviet Minister for Propaganda and Agitation, Ilychev, published an article which was clearly an attack on the Chinese position, explaining what was meant by co-existence and denouncing 'left-wing Communists' in tones which recalled and were intended to recall one of Lenin's most famous tracts: 'Left-wing Communism; an Infantile Disorder'.[4]

This pamphlet was an essay in sustained invective against all those Communists who were too proud, too stupid, too pedantic, or too honest to allow themselves room for manoeuvre. It was dedicated with savage irony to the prince of trimmers, David Lloyd-George, then Prime Minister of Britain. The chief offenders in Lenin's eyes were those German Communists who refused to soil their hands by entering parliament and joining established trade unions. It laid down a line which, advocated by anyone but Lenin, would have qualified as right-wing opportunism.

Lenin himself was then fighting for the very existence of the new Soviet system, and he had no intention of being particular about the methods used. 'Surely', he exclaimed in exasperation, 'the German Lefts cannot but know that the whole history of Bolshevism, both before and after the October Revolution, is *full* of instances of manoeuvring, temporizing, and compromising with other parties, bourgeois parties included!'

He went on to deliver what was to become the classic instructions for Bolshevik tactics:

To carry on a war for the overthrow of the international bourgeoisie, a war which is a hundred times more difficult and complicated than the most stubborn of ordinary wars between States, and to refuse beforehand to manoeuvre, to utilize the conflict of interests (even though temporary) among one's enemies, to refuse to temporize and compromise with possible allies (even though transient, unstable, vacillating, and conditional) – is this not ridiculous in the extreme? Is it not as though in the difficult ascent of an unexplored and hitherto inaccessible mountain we were to renounce beforehand the idea that at times we might have to go in zigzags, sometimes retracing our steps, sometimes giving up the course once selected and trying others?

And he went on with the famous passage which for decades was to serve as the blue-print to Communist duplicity, the battle order which lay behind all Stalin's more or less bloodless conquests in Europe (Communists, unlike some others, shed blood *after* they have conquered, not, if possible, in combat), achieved by the simple expedient of first cooperating with other parties, then swallowing them up:

It is possible to conquer the more powerful enemy only by exerting our efforts to the utmost and by *necessarily*, though carefully and attentively and skilfully, taking advantage of every 'fissure', however small, in the ranks of our enemies, of every antagonism of interests among the bourgeois of the various countries, among the various groups or types of bourgeoisie in the various countries; by taking advantage of every opportunity, however small, of gaining an ally among the masses, even though this ally be temporary, vacillating, unstable, unreliable, and conditional. Those who do not understand this, do not understand even a grain of Marxism and of scientific modern Socialism *in general*.

I cannot answer for 'scientific modern Socialism *in general*', but this has nothing whatever to do with Marxism. It has, however, everything to do with Leninism.

Comrade Ilychev did not quote those passages in his article. But they are the ones which spring into every good Communist's mind when he hears the phrase 'left-wing Communism'. 'Infantile Disorder' is the antiphon in the Communist litany. The fraternal comrades knew now what to think: the Chinese, who pitched into America headlong, who objected to Khrushchev's tactical manoeuvring, were being told that they were bad Marxists.

This article of Ilychev's was important. It represented the first formal effort by the Soviet Party to base its policy differences with China on the sacred writings of Lenin. And, in fact, pretty well everything that Khrushchev was to say and do thereafter could be justified by that text. It invited a reply, and in due course the reply was made, also based on the sacred writings: Marx and Lenin, like the Bible, can be made to prove different things, indeed quite contradictory things. In the months to come this convenience was to be fully exploited by both sides.

But during the rest of 1959 it was the Russians who were making the running and forcing the pace. In a speech to the Supreme Soviet on 30 October, Khrushchev, once more emphasizing the wrong-headedness of testing the strength of imperialism by force, made a moralizing reference to the case of Trotsky, which was clearly intended as a sharp rebuke to the Chinese. This was the first occasion on which the Chinese attitude was equated, though here very obliquely, with Trotskyism: later on this was to become a recurring feature of the dispute. Khrushchev also in that speech went out of his way to underline the Soviet attitude of neutrality in the Sino–Indian border dispute. And he made a new departure. He expressed his approval of de Gaulle's proposals for ending the Algerian war, a complete change of front. The Chinese went on attacking de Gaulle and doing their level best to encourage the F.L.N. to maintain a belligerent and intransigent attitude. Here was the first direct conflict in the matter of wars of liberation.

Then, on 1 December, at the Congress of the Hungarian Party in Budapest, Khrushchev attacked again. Privately, according to the Chinese, he freely criticized the communes and the Great Leap Forward to Congress delegates. This is not improbable: he had already uttered such criticism as far back as 1958, to an American senator of all people. And at Poznan in July 1959 he had spoken in a way which could only be taken as direct criticism of the commune system. Publicly he gave a pointed warning about comrades who were apt to become 'too conceited' and, indicating the existence of important differences within the Communist movement, said the Communist countries 'must synchronize their watches'. This was a phrase which was to be taken up by Pekin a little more than three years later, when the split had been publicly admitted by both sides. The question to be decided was, as the Chinese put it, whose watch told the right time?

Meanwhile the Chinese were sorting themselves out and preparing to take up the challenge. At meetings of the World Peace Council and the International Union of Students in January they themselves, besides opposing the Soviet line, lobbied energetically to win the support of fraternal parties, accusing the Russians of trying to isolate China in order to do a deal with the United States. This sort of behaviour, to be repeated even more forcefully at the Pekin meeting of the World Federation of Trade Unions early in June, was to form the basis of the formal Soviet charge of fractionalism.[5] The Chinese could reply, and did, that they were simply seeking to put forward their own point of view, which was being misrepresented by the Russians, and that the Russians, anyway, had themselves been lobbying hard. The fact remains that these 'underhand' (Khrushchev's phrase) activities shocked the leaders of many fraternal parties, to whom unilateral attempts to alter the Party line, unless by debate in full congress, were anathema. As we shall see, the Russians were able to exploit this mood most successfully at the Bucarest Congress later in June and at the great Moscow Conference in November. But for this behaviour the Chinese would have found more support at both meetings. It is an interesting commentary on the ossification of Communist thought and the power of Stalin's influence to live on long into the Khrushchev era that even the most anti-Stalinist leaders of the fraternal parties at first accepted Khrushchev's right to behave in a way which they condemned in the Chinese. It was not, indeed, until the end of the Moscow meeting that, by the boldest of counter-attacks, the Secretary General of the Chinese Communist Party, Teng Hsaio-ping, was able to question the very premises upon which Soviet overlordship rested – and sent many delegates home to their different countries in deep and troubled thought – though they had voted him down.

But before the Bucarest Conference more events occurred to add to the sharpness of the dispute. In February 1960 at a closed session of a meeting of the Warsaw Pact powers in Moscow (of the leaders of the European Communist countries, that is), Khrushchev delivered a comprehensive and extremely blunt attack on Chinese policies, while Marshal Konev made it plain, in so many words, that the Soviet Union had not the least intention of giving nuclear arms to China. In March the Soviet Party sent a formal invitation to the Chinese Party to send a party and governmental delegation to Moscow to discuss the differences that had arisen. The Russians did this, it is believed, in the teeth of advice from the Chinese prime minister, Chou En-lai, who has always been regarded by them as their friend. The Chinese refused the invitation, and in the following month opened their counter-offensive in earnest.

This was timed to coincide with the fortieth anniversary of Lenin's death, and it took the form of a series of articles in the Chinese press which lifted the dispute to a high ideological plane and for the first time indicated that Mao, not content with disputing with Khrushchev, was making a serious bid to snatch the leadership of the Communist movement from him.

The most important of these articles, which appeared in the Chinese Party fortnightly *Red Flag* on 16 April, was entitled 'Long Live Leninism'. This also is one of the documents which should be read by those who want to go more deeply into the dispute.[6] It is about 15,000 words long and would take up a quarter of this book if reproduced in full. As an essay in Marxist polemics it made not only the Ilychev article referred to above, but also the official Soviet reply to it, by the veteran Kuusinen, one of the few survivors from the Lenin era, look childish.[7] It was an elaborate, passionate, savage restatement of the Leninist position, utterly devoid of any spirit of compromise or live-and-let-live, wholly devoted to ways and means of achieving world revolution by the most direct available means in the shortest possible time. To the detached observer, and no doubt to some less detached, it echoes the raven-voiced accents of a reforming monk, a Savonarola rather than a Luther – but a Savonarola disposing of great temporal power and in a position to set himself up as an anti-pope.

The diatribe, or encyclical, opens with an evocation of the Paris Commune of 1848 as seen through the eyes of Karl Marx:

Even if the Commune should be destroyed, the struggle will only be postponed. The principles of Communism are perpetual and indestructible, they will present themselves again and again, until the working class is liberated.

Marx was thinking of Europe at the time of the industrial revolution. Mao was thinking of the teeming millions of Asia, the Middle East, Africa, and Latin America. The canvas is much larger. And it is because of the sheer size of this canvas that he could, throughout this tremendous manifesto, equate Khrushchev, unnamed, with the traitor to the revolution, Marshal Tito, without appearing ludicrous: Yugoslavia, to us, is small and insignificant compared with the Soviet Union; the Soviet Union to this pretender to the leadership of two-thirds of the population of the world is also small.

It is not necessary in this narrative to offer a detailed summary of 'Long Live Leninism'. The general trend of the argument has already emerged from these pages, and the detailed, concrete points of difference will pin-point themselves in subsequent chapters, especially those dealing with the Bucarest and Moscow conferences which took place later in 1960. It is a classic appeal, with strong evangelical overtones, not merely for the continuation of revolutionary activity but for accelerating it at a time when imperialism is in disarray in face of the oppressed of this world, rising in their hundreds of millions against their 'brutish' masters. It calls for the heightening of the revolutionary offensive all round, above all in the way of support to active Communists seeking by violence to overthrow the imperialist masters, or the bourgeois governments which were set up when the imperialists retreated. It applauds the principle of co-existence with capitalist countries, but co-existence seen as it was seen by Lenin – as a purely tactical expedient, pending the day when revolutionary hostility could openly declare itself. Meanwhile, all national revolution movements and all revolutionary uprisings in capitalist countries must be supported 'resolutely and without the least reservation'. As for war, so long as capitalism existed there would remain the very real danger of a major war. Communists must not flinch from this if it came, though they must seek to avoid it. Local wars, on the other hand, were bound to occur in the course of the revolutionary struggle and could only assist the progress of the revolution. As for violent revolution:

Revolution means the use of revolutionary violence by the oppressed class, it means revolutionary war. This is also true of the bourgeois revolutions. Lenin has put it well:

   History teaches us that no oppressed class ever achieved power, nor could achieve power, without going through a period of dictatorship, i.e. the conquest of political power and suppression by force of the most desperate, frenzied resistance offered by the exploiters.

And again, still quoting Lenin:

   Not a single great revolution in history has ever been carried out without a civil war and no serious Marxist will believe it possible to make the transition from capitalism to socialism without a civil war.

Thus the Chinese were now formally opposing Khrushchev on the three main points of his platform, and accusing him of revisionism, of 'betraying the revolution', of seeking to 'disarm the masses' and selling them to the imperialists. Co-existence; the non-inevitability of war; and revolution through peaceful means.

There was another point, which has been overlooked. After celebrating the Soviet superiority in rockets and weapons of destruction, seen as instruments to defeat the purposes of imperialist 'atomic blackmail', the article goes on to say

Never mind, Marxist-Leninists have always maintained that in world history it is not technique but men, the masses of people, that determine the fate of mankind. ... Comrade Mao Tse-tung has pointed out that the most abundant source of strength in war lies in the masses, and that a people's army organized by awakened and united masses of people would be invincible throughout the world.

Russians reading this little homily may well have reflected that they, as well as the Americans, were tending to rely on nuclear deterrents, and that it was the Chinese who had the masses.

A few days after the publication of the April articles the American U 2 was shot down over Sverdlovsk, and immediately after the immense uproar precipitated by this incident, Khrushchev proceeded to Paris, where he dramatically sabotaged the Summit Conference which he had striven for so mightily, and in the teeth of Chinese disapproval.

It was automatically assumed in the West that America had wrecked the Summit by her extraordinary behaviour in the spy-plane incident. It is impossible to be sure. There is no evidence at all that Pekin influenced Khrushchev directly in this matter; but he was at that time bracing himself for a final show-down with the Chinese, who in their April articles had in effect told the Communist movement that he was not fit to lead the Soviet Party, let alone the world Communist movement. ... He had already given a sign, in a speech in Baku in May, that he was shifting his ground about the Summit. 'It is no good having a Summit meeting', he declared, 'unless it settles the German question once and for all.' Since he knew very well that there was no possibility of the German question being settled, this had all the appearance of an escape route. And this impression was confirmed immediately after the Summit when Khrushchev went to East Berlin not to re-activate the German question but to tell Herr Ulbricht that he must wait patiently.

My own view is that Khrushchev was having second thoughts about the timing of the Summit: he wished to confront the Chinese as the man who was at least as anti-imperialist as they were. The U2 incident did two things: it very strongly re-inforced the Chinese case against the Americans in general and Eisenhower in particular, making Khrushchev's love affair with the American President look absurd; and it gave Khrushchev, who was certainly furious with Eisenhower, a chance to show Communists everywhere that when it came to anti-imperialist intransigence he was second to none.

But it did not deflect him from his long-term purpose, or from the three theses which the Chinese were challenging. Indeed, in a defence of his leisurely revolutionary programme he caused an article to be written in *Soviet Russia* on 10 June, in which the author, Shevlyagin, spoke of 'those terrible revolu-tionaries' who 'rush about trying to spread revolution before the time is ripe'.

10 June was also the last day of a meeting of the World Federation of Trade Unions in Pekin, where two Chinese speakers, one of them the Vice-Chairman of the W.F.T.U., Liu Chan-sheng, accused the Russians of insincerity in their dis-armament proposals, and where Chinese lobbying of delegates to influence them against the Russians was more marked than ever before.[8]

Ten days later the existence of the breach was finally declared and made public within the Communist movement at the fateful Congress of the Rumanian party in Bucarest, where Khrushchev himself faced the Chinese delegates and, with a great release of pent-up feeling, told them what he thought of them – and received as good as he gave.

Chapter Ten

THE BUCAREST CONFERENCE

WHEN the Third Congress of the Communist Party of Rumania opened on 20 June 1960, it appeared to the outside world as no more than a routine Congress of a minor Communist state. Indeed, this view was shared by most of the official delegates when they arrived in Bucarest. Very few of the parties outside the bloc sent their leaders, and it was not until 18 June, on the day of his departure from Moscow, that Khrushchev's own intention to attend the meeting was announced. This was almost certainly a last-minute decision induced by his failure the day before to make any headway with the Chinese delegation, headed by Peng Chen, when it called on him in Moscow on its way to Bucarest. But very few realized that it portended the opening of a major counter-attack on the Chinese position. Certainly the Chinese did not know this.

Peng was, and is, one of the first twelve in the Chinese Party hierarchy, tough and active and with a distinguished career behind him. As Mayor of Pekin and a member of the three main organs of party power, he was, and is, a force to be reckoned with in China. But at Bucarest he was heavily outranked not only by Khrushchev, but also by the East European party leaders, Gomulka and Novotny especially, who were also summoned to Bucarest at the last minute.

The Congress opened quietly enough. There were three days of open sessions, at which the various delegates made the sort of speeches that would have been expected. Khrushchev and Peng both spoke, mildly enough; but to the attentive ear it was clear that they were criticizing each other on the now familiar lines. Khrushchev, for example, attacked the 'mechanical repeaters of what Lenin had said about imperialism', dismissed such people as 'children', and had some hard things to say about the lack of understanding of those who could not see that war, 'under present circumstances', was not inevitable.

Peng for his part returned to the old thesis that imperialism can never be trusted, and was able to exploit the U2 incident and the fiasco of the Paris Summit meeting to underline his meaning. He stressed particularly those doctrinal points so often made by the Chinese which were in fact implicit criticism of the Soviet line. He particularly went out of his way to celebrate the struggles then raging in Algeria and Cuba, insisting that the best and surest way to avert war was to help liberation movements and revolutionary struggles everywhere. He returned vigorously to the familiar attack on Tito; the imperialists, he said, were using modern revisionists in their efforts to disrupt Communist unity. Most strikingly of all, he got through his whole speech without once referring to peaceful co-existence. To many of the assembled delegates this was one more round in a seemingly interminable game, or semi-public debate, between comrades who differed on points of emphasis and tactics. To the Russians it was a sign that the Chinese were still attacking hard. While Khrushchev sat back, or conferred privately with his chief European lieutenants, his team went into action.

His team consisted of B. Ponomarev and Y. A. Andropov, responsible for inter-Party relations between respectively the non-bloc Parties and the bloc Parties. Ponomarev had the most difficult task because he was dealing with delegates from all over the world, most of whom held Mao Tse-tung in the deepest respect and yet had no idea how far the cleavage had gone. Through half 22 and all 23 June he met groups of delegates privately and briefed them on the nature of the conflict and the Soviet position. These briefings were designed first to warn the fraternal delegates of the seriousness of the split, then to soften them up in order to make them the more receptive for the Soviet onslaught which was to follow. All the emphasis was placed on the opposed attitudes of Moscow and Pekin to war and co-existence, the Russians knowing very well that, no matter what reservations some of the fraternal Parties might have about Soviet attitudes in general, they were united in the fear of nuclear war. Indeed, ever since the dispute was formally laid before the world Communist movement in those June days at Bucarest the war-scare has been Khrushchev's trump card. Time and time again he has been able to conceal certain of the more fundamental differences, differences in which the Chinese view might be expected to win widespread sympathy among good Leninists, by invoking the spectre of nuclear destruction and reminding the comrades that the sort of recklessness displayed by the Chinese could all too easily unloose it on the world. And, remarkably, the Chinese, instead of counter-attacking by insisting (as they had every right to insist) to the exclusion of all else that they do not want a nuclear war, continued for a long time to play into Khrushchev's hands, as we shall see.

Apart from the issue of war and peace and co-existence, Ponomarev's main attack was on the Chinese way of handling the dispute – above all in their use of the W.F.T.U. meeting to make covert and uncomradely encroachments on the Soviet position, thus offending against one of the first laws of the Communist movement – that all disputes and debates must be confined to strictly Party circles.

Having prepared the way, Ponomarev produced for each of the groups he addressed copies of a circular letter, specially prepared for the consumption of all delegates to the Congress, in which the shortcomings of the Chinese were elaborately set out. Since this eighty-page letter represented, as far as is known, the first presentation of the Soviet case against China in any sort of detail intended for the eyes of senior Party members alone (the public speeches and press articles referred to hitherto were, of course, available to all the world, and had to be worded accordingly), it is worth recording in some detail the sense of what it said. It was a criticism mainly of Chinese ideas, but also to some extent of Chinese behaviour. It made the 1957 Moscow Declaration a touchstone and accused the Chinese of departing from the ideology enshrined in that document, just as the Chinese themselves were to accuse the Russians of precisely the same conduct.

After a brief historical summary, which took in certain of the points already dealt with in this narrative, and stressed above all China's unfriendly attitude as expressed in the Lenin anniversary articles and her conduct in the W.F.T.U. and other international organizations, the argument opened with a discussion of the 'character of the present era'. As Khrushchev himself was later to say, this was a question of fundamental importance. The reason for this was that Communists cannot act until they have, as it were, agreed on the precise historical location of the moment in which they find themselves. Is it an epoch marked by the decline of imperialism or the rise of imperialism? Is it an epoch in which revolutionaries are fighting for their very existence, or one in which the revolutionary movement has become so strong, commanding popular support on such a scale, that it can move forward with controlled moderation to a predetermined end? And so on. In the not-far-distant past such definitions were promulgated by Stalin, and there was no answering back.

Now, in their circular letter of 21 June, the Russians declared that the Chinese had come forward with their own formulation and that it was false. They had defined the present epoch as one of 'imperialism, wars, and revolutions'. But this was only half the story, for it failed to recognize changes in the balance of world forces. The present 'epoch' was also marked by the 'disintegration of imperialism, transition to Socialism, and of formation and consolidation of the world system of Socialism'. It was of extreme importance that this Soviet formulation be recognized as correct; it was bound up with the strategy and tactics to be followed by the movement as a whole – strategy and tactics which now found their proper expression in the concepts of peaceful transition to Socialism, peaceful co-existence, and the correct line on war, peace, and disarmament. The Chinese formulation made nonsense of this line.

The circular then went on to consider the various aspects of strategy and tactics one by one. The Chinese, it said, had once subscribed to Khrushchev's peaceful co-existence thesis. But lately they had gone back on it. In *Red Flag* they had gone so far as to say that it was only the 'imperialist general staff' which could decide whether there would be war or peace, and that Communists had no say in the matter. Such a statement was based on a faulty analysis of the forces existing in the world today. It was wrong to think of war as being a purely economic phenomenon. There were such strong forces working for peace that these could well be sufficient in themselves to stop the imperialists from resorting to war. The most decisive factor in this relationship of forces was the strength of the Socialist camp. To talk of the inevitability of war was an invitation to 'fatalism'. It not only minimized the strength of the Socialist camp but 'paralysed the revolutionary struggle' by inducing in the people a spirit of despair, thus 'disarming them in advance'.

Mao himself had once believed this, the circular continued. At the 1957 Moscow Conference he himself had said: 'Everything reduces itself to gaining fifteen years. Lasting peace will then be assured throughout the world.' But now the Chinese showed inconsistency. In one breath they called imperialism a 'paper tiger', in the next that they saw that the imperialists could not be restrained.

The Chinese were saying that those who believed that war can be averted were opposed to wars of liberation. This was untrue. Indeed, the class struggle would intensify once the threat of war had been eliminated, and co-existence did not in any way involve the renunciation of the struggle for national liberation, 'including armed struggle'. Peaceful co-existence simply meant 'gaining time' for the 'consolidation of the Socialist system and the acceleration of the building of Socialism and Communism'. It encouraged centrifugal forces within the 'imperialist bloc' and all the time sharpened contradictions within individual imperialist countries and between them. It was impossible to accept the arguments put forward by *Red Flag* to the effect that 'we need not fear war' and that the losses suffered in war would be compensated for by the victory of Socialism. 'The Communist Parties cannot permit society to be thrown back hundreds of years' or the destruction of 'hundreds of millions' of people.

The circular then went on to deal with the charge that by its policies towards the uncommitted the Soviet Party was 'flirting with the national bourgeoisie' and 'abandoning class positions'. This was totally false. Soviet economic aid to the 'liberated' countries was justified by the fact that such aid promoted the cause of peace and weakened imperialism. The Chinese now objected to this policy because, they said, as the national bourgeois gain power they themselves tend to become imperialists – for example India, the U.A.R., and Indonesia. But all good Communists should know that it is vitally important not to 'skip stages in the revolution'. It was necessary to increase their friends among the neutralists and to support neutralist governments; only imperialism would profit from internecine strife in the national liberation movements.

As for disarmament, the Chinese objections to the call for disarmament, namely that it encouraged 'illusions' among the masses, was based on a failure to appreciate the real meaning of the Soviet proposals. This was that by concentrating on disarmament the creation of broad popular fronts and mass movements in favour of peace would be facilitated, thus embarrassing 'bellicose circles' in their efforts to intensify the arms race. One of the major Soviet aims in the disarmament campaign was to get rid of U.S. overseas bases. The Chinese line could lead only to a continuation of the cold war and of the arms race. It would, moreover, obstruct the peace policies of the Soviet Union by appearing to give substance to the claims of the imperialists that Communists believe in war and want it.

Finally, the circular flatly rebutted Chinese charges that the Soviet Party was insisting that the 'peaceful way' to Socialism was the only way. Both at the 20th Party Congress in Moscow and at the Moscow Conference in 1957 the 'peaceful way' had been put forward as one way among others. The Chinese had accepted this thesis. If they had now changed their minds they should say so openly.

This, in sum, was Moscow's formal exposure of the ideological differences, supported by a great deal of repetitive argument. The main points were to be echoed again and again in the months to come, not only in direct polemics with the Chinese, but in countless commentaries and leading articles in the world Communist press. But never in any subsequent public utterance was Khrushchev's motivation to be so sharply revealed – above all the motives he gave for his disarmament campaign: to capture popular support throughout the world among all those longing for peace, to turn the masses against the governments, and thus to embarrass the West in its defence efforts and to make it increasingly hard for America to keep her overseas bases. This sort of argument had to be reserved for Communist ears alone.

The remainder of the circular was on a lower plane. It contained the first attack on Chinese behaviour as distinct from Chinese ideology. And although this attack was to be pressed much harder both at Bucarest and in Moscow later in the year, the circular letter gave the first indication that the conflict between Moscow and Pekin was by no means purely ideological, but was also bound up with great-power jealousies and resentments.

Thus the circular accused the Chinese of 'insincerity' and of 'violating the principles of proletarian internationalism' by their equivocal behaviour in insisting that the Soviet Union must be the acknowledged leader of the Socialist camp, while covertly attacking the Soviet Party on the side, either by implication (as in the Lenin anniversary articles) or, more heinously, by lobbying delegates to international conferences. In contrast to this sort of behaviour, the circular declared, Soviet conduct had been beyond reproach. Even when the Soviet Party had disagreed with Chinese policies – as, for instance, the 'Hundred Flowers' interlude and the introduction of the communes – it had studiously refrained from intervening. 'Loyalty to Leninism', the circular continued rather pompously, 'is measured not only by words but by deeds.' Had not the Soviet Union assisted China to the tune of 5 billion roubles in goods and 6·6 billion roubles in credits ? (The Chinese were later to retort that they themselves had distributed among deserving cases just as much material aid as they had ever received from Moscow.)

After a sharp reference to China's apparent desire to question Moscow's handling of the personality cult, which the whole movement had regarded as being settled long ago, the circular concluded by saddling Pekin with the blame for weakening the unity of the Communist movement. What was worse, she had rejected comradely criticism. Khrushchev himself had spent a long time personally arguing with the Chinese delegation in Moscow only a few days earlier. But to no avail. The only solution was to call a meeting of all Communist Parties in order to thresh the matter out.

So much for the circular letter of 21 June. It was stiff in tone, sometimes extremely blunt, but always closely argued. It came as a deep shock to most of the delegates to realize that the two greatest parties in the Communist movement were very seriously at loggerheads on points of basic policy. But there was nothing in the letter to prepare them for the violence and emotionalism that was to come. I have summarized this letter rather fully not only for the light it casts on some aspects of the dispute – a far more vivid illumination was soon to be supplied by the speeches of Khrushchev and Peng Cheng – but, and more particularly, because it is the first private document we have which purports to set out, not for Western consumption, but for the secret guidance of embattled comrades, the true nature and meaning of Khrushchev's international policies. Such insights are exceedingly rare. Later on we shall have to discuss the very big question of just how much this intimate document expressed Khrushchev's true thoughts about Communist strategy, and to what extent, if any, he was concealing these in order to make propaganda inside the Party against the Chinese, just as he habitually makes propaganda outside the Party against, say, the Americans. But that must wait. For the time being it will be convenient to take the letter as a faithful reflection of Soviet strategy and aims.

While Ponomarov was feverishly engaged in indoctrinating the fraternal parties outside the bloc, and while the delegates were busy digesting the eighty pages of the circular letter, the Congress continued, and there was nothing on the surface to indicate the turmoil behind the scenes. But on 25 June, after the final session of the Congress proper, the private meeting called by the Russians was convened and got under way. It was soon clear that Ponomarov and Andropov had done their work well. The speakers were limited to twenty minutes each, and all day, one after another, delegates from all over the world got up in support of the official communiqué (which Peng had refused to sign until he had consulted with Pekin), and against the Chinese positions as interpreted by the Russians: Figuères of France, Bikdash of Syria, Alberdi of the Argentine, Colombi of Italy, Kerrigan of Britain, Japan, East Germany, Spain, Iran, Morocco, Uruguay, Belgium, Chile, Finland, the United States (in the person of Miss Elizabeth Flynn), all monotonously appealed for unity and either questioned the Chinese, their methods, and their policies, or criticized them more or less sharply. Peng Chen, representative of a proud and ancient civilization, had to sit and listen to the Arab, Bikdash, of Syria begging him to use his brains and to learn how to be helpful. . . .

The fraternal parties seemed to be doing Moscow's work for it. When Peng himself spoke he was clearly taken aback by the weight of opinion against China; but he was remarkably restrained. He had listened attentively to much criticism of the

Chinese Party, he said, and would bring it to the attention of the Central Committee. Nevertheless, he had to say at once that he considered much of the criticism unjust. Only part of the truth had been revealed, and the Chinese view-point had nowhere been expressed. He must ask the delegates to familiarize themselves with the real views of the Chinese Party. He denied that the Chinese were in any way opposed to co-existence: they practised it themselves. He said that the trouble with the W.F.T.U. had arisen because it had tried to ridicule the industrial and agricultural progress of China, and this had led to 'a disagreeable situation'. As for peace and war, of course the Chinese had always favoured the struggle for peace. Hadn't they supported Khrushchev's visit to the U.S. and the position he had maintained at the Summit meeting in Paris? But he himself could not agree to the view that the imperialists would not start another war. The Americans, he said, were certainly not arming Japan and West Germany just to join in the May Day celebrations with the Chinese. This meant that China must always be prepared to prevent war and confront the enemy. This, he said, was in full accordance with the Moscow Declaration of 1957.

When Peng sat down the general situation appeared to be well under control. But something else had happened on that day, which angered Khrushchev exceedingly. As a counter-move to the earlier circulation of the Soviet letter of 21 June criticizing the Chinese, Peng had produced a document of his own. This was a translation, running to more than eighty pages, of a *private* letter from the Soviet Party to the Chinese Party, and its publication to the assembled delegates threw quite a new light on Soviet attitudes and methods. The letter of 21 June had been composed especially to carry conviction with the fraternal parties. It was, as we have seen, a dignified and reasoned statement cast in Leninist terms; and, though sometimes surprisingly blunt, it was nowhere abusive. The speakers at the first closed meeting had taken their tone from this letter: they were engaged in a seemly debate.

But this private letter, intended for Chinese eyes alone, was something quite other. In tone it was hectoring and bitter, in construction loose and wide-ranging (like one of Khrushchev's own speeches). Far from expressing itself in terms of conventional Leninist polemic (which can itself be bitter and abusive enough), and trying to sustain the argument on a high ideological plane, it threw in all sorts of charges, some of them having nothing to do with ideological differences, but rather with power relationships and inter-state rivalries. It directly attacked Chinese policy towards India and Algeria. It said that Chinese actions were destroying all confidence in the bourgeois world in the Communist desire for peace and, to make matters worse, were making the peoples of Asia and Africa highly suspicious of Communism. It attacked the Chinese for being nationalists before they were Communists, and it bitterly charged them with a refusal to cooperate fully in military matters with the Soviet Union. It was, in a word, the explosion of an angry father faced with a rebellious son. It showed up in the most startling way the seamy side of Moscow's attitude towards Pekin, and its publication to the fraternal delegates seriously undermined the impression the Russians had been so sedulously striving to create – that they were arguing with the Chinese more in sorrow than in anger, more in bewilderment than in bitterness.

It was almost certainly the publication of this letter that made Khrushchev himself decide to intervene next day. That evening the secret session was broken off so that the final public act of the Congress could be staged. It was a mass occasion. Harmless and amicable speeches were made. The Communist movement had never been so united. Khrushchev himself at a reception later that evening was in tremendous form. As far as the outside world was concerned, the 3rd Rumanian Congress was coming to an end with expressions of mutual esteem between delegates representing the united Communist Parties of the world and the Communist governments of countries containing more than a third of the population of the world.

But behind the scenes there was doubting in the hearts of many of the fêted delegates, fury in the hearts of the Russians, modified triumph in the hearts of the Chinese – who, by publishing the Soviet letter, had managed to put the record straight from their point of view and start the fraternal comrades asking questions: were the Russians, was Khrushchev, quite so patently in the right as they had tried to make out? They remembered that Russian Communists had been known to err before. They remembered Stalin. . . . Khrushchev, behind his affability, was conscious of all this. He also knew that publication of this purely private communication (an old Soviet trick, now turned against the Russians themselves, and by Communists) was not a sudden, spontaneous gesture. It could only have been done on the authority of the Chinese Politburo, and it could not have been done at all had the translation not been prepared in Pekin well before the Chinese delegation had set out for Bucarest, pretending that they had no idea that there was to be any public discussion of the differences.

Knowing all this, he decided that an all-out attack was the only answer. And this, after listening to a few more speeches at the second closed session next day, he delivered.

Even by Khrushchev's standards (he had just come back from his notorious press conference at the break-up of the Paris Summit) it was an extraordinary performance. He had in front of him a prepared speech, but, as so often on lesser occasions, it was soon clear that he was departing from that speech and, carried away (but nobody knows just how much Khrushchev is ever carried away; how much his seeming indiscretions are deliberately calculated), was improvising as he went along.

He did not observe the twenty-minute rule – which Peng had punctiliously adhered to. He abandoned reasoned argument and, indeed, all pretence of judicious analysis of differences and embarked on a violent tirade couched in purely personal terms which was foreign not only to the spirit of Marxist-Leninism but also to the spirit of great power diplomacy.

He had only decided to speak, he said, because the representative of the Chinese Party had himself spoken. He had to make it clear that what was at issue was not simply a disagreement between the Soviet and the Chinese Parties, but a disagreement between the Chinese Party on the one hand and all the other Parties on the other. The smaller Parties had as much right to be heard as the larger ones. He attacked Mao Tse-tung by name, saying that he was in effect another Stalin, 'oblivious of any interests other than his own, spinning theories detached from the realities of the modern world'. He had become 'an ultra Leftist, an ultra dogmatist, indeed, a *left revisionist*'. The Chinese, he said, talked a great deal about war, but in fact they simply did not understand the meaning of modern war. He had a great deal to say about the frontier dispute with India, rejecting violently the Chinese charge that the Russians had let them down by refusing to support them. In fact, it had been the Chinese who had let the cause of Socialism down. By quarrelling with the Government of India they had not merely failed to work with the Russians towards the socialization of India; they had worked against it. Of course Nehru was a capitalist. But the Chinese dispute with him had nothing to do with capitalism and Socialism: it was a purely nationalist dispute and it had done the Socialist cause untold harm, quite apart from such details as losing Kerala to Communism. What right had Peng to complain of lack of support in such circumstances, especially when anyway it was impossible to get at the rights and wrongs of the dispute? Why, moreover, should the Chinese, who were always boasting of their colossal population, need support from the Soviet Union, whose population was less than the population of India? And what would happen to this frontier dispute when the day came, as it would, when India was a Socialist country? The Chinese comrades, he said, should take to heart what Lenin had said about great nation chauvinism. They should also remember that it had been Lenin who was prepared to surrender territory for tactical reasons – as under the Treaty of Brest Litovsk – and Trotsky who had opposed any abandonment of territory. Meanwhile Nehru had become a national hero, and this was just what the imperialists desired. The Soviet Union too had her frontier problems. But she approached these in a responsible way. If she had taken the Chinese line, war would have been declared on Iran more than once. There had been plenty of border incidents on the Russo–Iranian frontier, and men had been killed in them. But the Soviet Union would not allow incidents of this kind to precipitate war, since this would contradict the true spirit of revolution.

He attacked the Chinese for calling in question the whole attack on the personality cult. He lifted a small corner of the veil over Sino–Soviet military cooperation when he complained bitterly that the Chinese had hampered Soviet defence measures on the Manchurian border by preventing the installation of a radio transmitter 'for use against our enemies' and hindering reconnaissance flights by Soviet aircraft.

But his greatest contempt and bitterness was reserved for Chinese methods of controversy and Chinese domestic expedients. The Chinese were trying to force their views on others, he said. The methods they used in the matter of the W.F.T.U. were purely Trotskyite in kind. And yet they 'sent Peng Teh-huai to a Labour camp' because he had dared criticize the policy of the communes in a letter to the C.P.S.U. The Russians did not agree with the communes, nor with the Great Leap Forward. But they had not said so. They thought the 'Hundred Flowers' policy had been mistaken. But they had not said so. Development of a country's economy had to be regular, not in leaps and bounds. He added, interestingly, that strikes had occurred in Russia as a result of trying to force the pace.

After this extraordinary performance Peng got up to reply in kind; and this he did with far more elegance and real bite than Khrushchev had displayed.

It was now clear, he said, that Khrushchev had organized the meeting for the sole purpose of attacking the Chinese Party and Mao Tse-tung and to cover up a Soviet effort to undermine the prestige of the Chinese Party. As for Mao being remote from reality, in fact he was far more closely in touch with the modern world than Khrushchev. He, Khrushchev, was the revisionist, creating illusions about the true nature of imperialism and under-estimating its real strength. The Chinese Party did not at all trust his analysis of the general situation. As for his policy – what, anyway, was it? He sharply attacked Khrushchev's habit of blowing now hot now cold toward the imperialist powers – a tactic which seriously compromised the struggle of the masses. In a passage which arouses fellow feeling in our breasts he challenged his audience to deduce from Soviet actions what Soviet policy really was. As for understanding modern war, the Chinese had proved in Korea as well as against the Japanese that they had more experience than any other people in the world.

Khrushchev did not reply. The gauntlet was down. The extreme personal bitterness between Khrushchev and Mao was revealed, and the revelation had to be pondered on and digested. There were a few more speeches, some (notably the speech of the

Bulgarian, Zhivkov) fulsome in Khrushchev's praise, some less fulsome. But nobody, nobody at all apart from the Albanians, spoke up for the Chinese. The joint communiqué was finally signed, and it was agreed that there should be a conference of all the Parties in Moscow in November, to coincide with the celebrations of the anniversary of Lenin's revolution. A Commission was set up to prepare for this conference, and the delegates went off home with plenty to think about. They had assisted not at a rational discussion of certain doctrinal differences between the two senior parties, which was what the meeting had at first promised to be, but at a head-on collision between two parties contending for Lenin's inheritance – or between two great powers who happened to be Communist.

At the time the outside world knew nothing about this. The communiqué was carefully designed to conceal what had happened. It was not until two months after the November conference that we learnt what had happened at Bucarest. But between the two conferences, it was perfectly plain, Sino–Soviet relations were going from bad to worse.

Chapter Eleven

THE BATTLE DEVELOPS

I

FROM the little we know of them, the reports circulated among their flocks by the delegates of the various fraternal parties on their return home gave a fairly accurate idea of the main grounds of dispute but did not publicize the recriminatory aspects of Khrushchev's and Peng's speeches. Enough was known, however, for rank-and-file Communists to follow more intelligently the progress of the conflict as it was faintly (but largely accurately) mirrored in the Soviet and Chinese press, and to cause many among them – even those who were most frightened of Chinese belligerence in the nuclear age – to nourish reservations about some of Khrushchev's attitudes.

Almost at once – on 29 June – *Pravda* in Moscow and *People's Daily* in Pekin carried editorials on the Bucarest communiqué which indicated clearly that the Soviet and Chinese positions were as far apart as ever. In July Khrushchev took his first action against the Chinese by stopping publication of the Chinese–Russian journal *Friendship* in Moscow on the ground that it had carried offensive editorials. In the same month the Moscow party journal *Communist* attacked Chinese positions (without mentioning the name of China) more sharply than ever before. 'Only doctrinaires, not revolutionaries', could fail to understand the significance of peaceful co-existence in the 'changed circumstances' of today. Those who argue that co-existence 'could disarm the peoples ideologically and demobilize them' are guilty of misleading certain parties. 'They can only drag these parties to sectarianism and dogmatism.' Anyone who takes action to create disunity in the bloc is willy-nilly working against the success of the struggle for peace and socialism'. A few days later the Central Committee of the Soviet Party issued a resolution which put the final stamp on earlier press attempts to make it appear, falsely, that the Bucarest Congress had formally endorsed Khrushchev's policies (the theses of the 20th and 21st Party

Congresses), and that this endorsement had included a denunciation of 'narrow nationalism'. For the first time, too, ideas which the Chinese were known to hold were formally characterized as 'deviations'.

Behind the scenes, meanwhile, the affair of the Soviet technicians was boiling up. The Soviet Party wrote to Pekin complaining formally of the Chinese attitude towards Soviet technicians. The Soviet Union, the letter said, had wanted to withdraw these technicians for work at home some years earlier, on the grounds that enough Chinese technicians had then been trained. The Chinese had demurred and the technicians had stayed on. Later the Chinese had complained about the behaviour of some of them and once more the Soviet Union had proposed to withdraw them. Once more the Chinese had demurred – only to start a campaign of subversion by circulating 'anti-Marxist' pamphlets among them. Within a week Moscow wrote again saying that all Soviet technicians would be withdrawn in August.

This was a body blow to the Chinese. The technicians were those charged with the building of factories equipped by the Russians. When they left they took with them not only their skills, but also their blue-prints, without which the Chinese could not proceed. The heat was being turned on, not as between parties but as between states. The Chinese reacted sharply, not only rebutting the Soviet charges, but objecting especially to Soviet methods. Any Soviet complaints, they said, could be discussed; but there could not be unilateral action by the Russians. Such action was a violation of the Sino–Soviet treaty. It would damage China's construction programme, create all sorts of difficulties, weaken the bloc, and give comfort to the imperialists. A more concrete reply was the Chinese boycotting of a grand conference of orientologists which opened in Moscow on 9 August. Nobody could miss the significance of this, because the conference had been widely publicized and it was to be largely about Sinology.

The press campaign continued. Li Fu-chu in an article in *Red Flag* on 16 August declared that the 'modern revisionists' who had been trying to isolate China since 1958 would end up by isolating themselves.

On almost the same day, Li Wei-han made a speech in which

for the first time it was formally asserted that the Chinese were the only correct interpreters of Leninism, and that the 'Mao Tse-tung ideology is Marxist-Leninism in its fullest developed form'. He also stated uncompromisingly that 'armed struggle is the principal form of waging the revolution'. It was interesting that this speech was not published until a month later.

But the main Chinese counter-attack came in yet another letter dated 10 September addressed by the Chinese to the Soviet Party, which was a direct and detailed reply to the Soviet letter of 21 June already summarized. It was a serious attempt to put the whole dispute into perspective, and it formed the base of the Chinese position as it was to be exposed at the Moscow Conference in November.

This letter opened by stating that the conflict of views was not recent, as the Russians had pretended. It went back to the 20th Party Congress in 1956. Then, the Chinese said, the Soviet Party had wrongfully ignored Stalin's 'positive role' without previous discussion with the fraternal parties. At the same time, and also without consultation, it had put forward a false theory of 'peaceful transition'. The Chinese Party at the time had registered its objection both to the decisions and in the unilateral way they had been taken.

There had been further differences. It was in this letter that the Chinese first declared that it had been they who had advised the Russians against using armed force in Poland, and also against calling a meeting of the fraternal parties to condemn the Polish Party; further, that it had been they who had 'been obliged to intervene' to ensure the crushing of the Hungarian uprising by force.

The letter then went on to insist that there had been differences at the Moscow Conference in 1957, when the Chinese Party had been successful in forcing significant revisions to the first draft of the twelve-party declaration, particularly with regard to the pursuit of revolution. Then, having reminded the Soviet Party that at the Moscow Conference Mao had insisted that the Russians were the leaders of the Communist bloc, and that leadership carried certain responsibilities, the letter went on to set out, point by point, the Chinese ideological position. It was, in effect, a supreme attempt by Pekin to restore the debate to the high and comparatively dispassionate level on which it had proceeded until decorum had been exploded by Khrushchev's Bucarest tirade. It was an attempt to tell the fraternal comrades what the dispute was really about, in Marxist terms. It was very long.

On 2 June, the letter said, the Soviet Party had written to the Chinese Party calling for an international meeting to resolve differences. The Chinese had agreed, but asked for time to prepare themselves. On 7 June the Soviet Party had suggested a preliminary conference at Bucarest to discuss tactics following the collapse of the Paris Summit. It was to be a private meeting, and, the Russians had said, there would be no formal resolution. The Chinese had agreed. But Khrushchev had taken them wholly by surprise by launching a full-scale attack for which they were not prepared. Instead of pursuing the campaign against imperialism, as proposed, Khrushchev had started a 'harmful and disruptive' attack on the Chinese Party. Did the Soviet Party have any idea of how much this conduct had damaged Soviet prestige as leader of the bloc?

The rest of the letter covered familiar ground. There was only one moment of light relief. Khrushchev had derided Mao's 'paper tiger' thesis, but what about Lenin, who himself had said 'Anglo–French imperialism has feet of clay'. This absurdity was to rumble on and on until, in December 1962, *Pravda* was solemnly to define the difference between paper tigers and feet of clay, once and for all time. . . .

The Chinese Party letter of 10 September was a direct challenge to Khrushchev's position, and Khrushchev had to take action accordingly. The fraternal comrades knew that there were deadly serious issues at stake – and here were the Chinese discussing them more soberly and rationally than the Russians. Here, too, was a revelation that the very existence of the bloc had been saved by Mao at the time of the Polish and Hungarian rebellions. It was not enough for Khrushchev to bluster away; he had to work hard to justify his position. The one fatal weakness in the Chinese case was the fact that Mao had not in 1956 openly objected to the resolutions of the 20th Party Congress.

This lent an air of disingenuousness to some aspects of the Chinese case. Why could they not plainly admit that there had been a great change of mind in Pekin in 1957–8? The answer, almost certainly, is that the Chinese change of mind sprang primarily from an irrepressible explosion of nationalist arrogance and pride which would have been impossible to justify in Leninist terms. At Bucarest Peng Chen had said nothing at all to indicate the existence of deep national grievances. But as the preparations for the Moscow Conference took shape these grievances began to show through. The first was the affair of the Soviet technicians, which clearly went back a long way. The second was when, for the first time in front of other Parties, the Chinese complained – and with great bitterness – that the Russians had refused to support them over Formosa and to give them nuclear weapons. . . .

2

Twenty-six parties were represented on the preparatory commission, which met in Moscow towards the end of September (after the Chinese letter of 10 September had been circularized to all parties). The Soviet members were Kozlov and Suslov, and the Chinese sent a thirteen-man delegation headed by Teng Hsiao-ping, Secretary-General of the Chinese Party, small, bullet-headed, tough, and one of the most determined proponents of Pekin's stand against Moscow. With him in support was Peng Chen, who had already exchanged salvoes with Khrushchev at Bucarest. These two were to hold the fort against Suslov and Kozlov during the preparatory stages before the Conference opened, when Liu Shao-chi, the Chairman of the People's Republic, or Prime Minister, and Mao Tso-tung's putative successor, arrived to lead the Chinese delegation.

Teng started off as he meant to go on. The task of the Commission was to produce a document, a new policy declaration which was to reinforce, or supersede, the declaration of 1957 and in its text reconcile once and for all the differing viewpoints so that the Communist Parties of the world could speak with a unified voice. Since the final document, when it was published in December, was extremely long, and since the Chinese argued about every paragraph, it was no wonder that the preparatory commission sat more or less continuously from late September

until early November. They argued because the draft document
had been prepared by the Russians (somebody had to prepare it,
and the Chinese were still making a great show of regarding the
Russians as the leading party). And they argued with extreme
acrimony and animosity. It was, indeed, during this discussion
that many of the foreign delegates learned for the first time that
one of the real causes of Chinese bitterness and the frequent
stressing in the Chinese press of the necessity for 'going it alone'
and not relying on outside help had been Khrushchev's refusal
to give China nuclear weapons. The Chinese were clearly determined to work their own point of view into every paragraph of
the document, and both sides were tireless in repeating *ad
nauseam* the charges with which we are already familiar. Western
diplomats, politicians, and functionaries who have to negotiate
with Russians may take comfort from the thought that Soviet
stubbornness and repetitiveness is not reserved for capitalists.
The Chinese received the full treatment, and they gave as good
as they got.

Two points in particular led to almost interminable wrangling
– one almost incidental, the other going to the very heart of
things. The incidental point was the Chinese resistance to any
form of words critical of the cult of personality which might
conceivably be construed as a criticism of their own cult of Mao,
now withdrawn from public office and, as it were, presiding over
China like a cloud-born deity. The vital point referred to the
business of fractionalism: the Chinese refused point blank to
countenance a paragraph condemning fractionalism, on the
grounds that this was a barely concealed attack on what the
Russians chose to regard, erroneously, as their own disruptive
activities in front organizations. This wrangle was to dominate
the conference itself, until finally Teng, in his great anti-
Khrushchev oration, came out into the open in what as we shall
see was one of the most dramatic moments in the history of the
world Communist movement.

But somehow, with infinite pains, some sort of an agreed text
(with strong reservations from the Chinese) was drawn up in
time for the opening of the Conference proper. In an article
dated 19 December, Signor Longo (who led the Italian delegation in Togliatti's absence and made perhaps the most important

speech of the whole meeting) said that most of the differences had been ironed out by the Preparatory Commission in the course of a discussion that was 'detailed and frank'. He said that 'only a few questions were left open for discussion in full conference'. He did not say that at the banquet which closed the proceedings Khrushchev and Teng Hsaio-ping were involved in a violent slanging match when Khrushchev protested strongly against certain of Teng's remarks denigrating the role which the Soviet Party had played in the Communist movement. He did not say that the points left open for discussion were vital in the extreme – above all whether or not the declaration was to mention fractionalism.

The outside world knew nothing of all this at the time. It knew well enough that there was growing friction between the Soviet Union and China, reflected in the veiled press polemics, the reiterated statements of views which could not be reconciled, and reports of the withdrawal of Soviet technicians. But about the background it had nothing firm to go on, and it was easy for those who, for whatever reason, wished to minimize the conflict to talk about a family quarrel. The outside world knew that delegates from Communist Parties from all over the world were collecting in Moscow on the occasion of the forty-fifth anniversary of Lenin's revolution. It knew that some sort of a conference must be going on behind closed doors. But there was nothing to show just what was being discussed. I myself believed, and wrote, that what appeared to be going on was a high policy discussion in which some of Khrushchev's colleagues, working with the Chinese, were bringing pressure to bear on Khrushchev to change his policies. It never crossed my mind that the pressure was coming from the Chinese alone (unless you count the Albanians), and that they alone, by standing up to Moscow, had put not only Khrushchev but the united Soviet Government heavily on the defensive, so that they had had to call in all the comrades from all over the world to declare themselves.

*

From the point of view of the Russians the Conference proper began unhappily. The scale of the meeting can be gathered from the fact that 108 delegates made speeches in the course of 33 sessions. Eighty-one of the 87 Communist Parties were represented, and all but the parties of China, North Korea, Japan, Indonesia, and Italy were represented by their leaders. But as this extraordinary gathering of Communists began to assemble in Moscow they found to their deep indignation that they were being treated in the way the Russians know so well how to treat foreigners of every kind – not as brothers, but as suspicious objects. Each delegation was cooped up in its own hotel rooms, and the Russian hosts went to great pains and considerable lengths to ensure that they did not mingle unless under direct Soviet surveillance: many of the delegations wanted to get together among themselves in order to discuss their attitudes to the terrible dispute between Pekin and Moscow; but the Russians were having none of this. To make matters worse the delegates were submitted to a process of indoctrination which amounted, really, to pressurizing. As in Bucarest, but to a much greater degree, high Soviet Party functionaries were told off to tackle each delegation in turn in order to put the Soviet point of view and make sure that the unfortunate delegates were thinking along the right lines. Most of the emphasis in these preliminaries seems to have been on Chinese lack of good faith: the Russians, to put the delegates in the right mood, stressed every point they could seize upon to demonstrate that, whatever the rights and wrongs of the Chinese viewpoint as such, Pekin had been behaving in an underhand and uncomradely manner. The W.F.T.U. episode was played to the limit, and there were some interesting sidelights on the withdrawal of the Soviet technicians from China. There had been some spectacular ructions between the Russians and the Chinese, who had blamed Soviet technicians for the premature wearing out of machinery and publicly burned Soviet blue-prints. When the technicians were finally withdrawn, the Chinese had given them white flags, a traditional Chinese gesture of contempt.

All in all many of the delegates were in a very troubled mood. They were not only being treated by the Russians like dangerous foreigners; they were now being treated like children and subjected to a schoolboy whispering campaign instead of to serious argument. If the Chinese had played their cards more skilfully when the conference proper opened they would have found many of the delegates in an extremely receptive mood.

Things looked up a little when Suslov himself took a hand. This he did in a commentary to the draft declaration, which was given to every delegate. This commentary put with unusual concision and briskness the main ideological points at issue between Moscow and Pekin, and contained no reference at all to inter-State frictions. Although Suslov's commentary contained nothing new, it put out so clearly the ground upon which the Russians proposed to take their stand that it is worth summarizing here:

(1) The Chinese do not understand the changes which have taken place in the relationship between political and economic forces and have incorrectly interpreted the principles of Lenin.

(2) The Russians believe that the forces of Socialism are strong enough to prevent war. The Chinese, earlier, maintained that fifteen years of peace would permit the total elimination of war. They have now abandoned this idea and say that the capitalists cannot be prevented from making war.

(3) The Chinese nominally support peaceful co-existence; but at the same time they say that war is inevitable. There are only two possible ways – war or peace. There is no third way. The Soviet Union cannot allow the capitalists to destroy humanity. Peaceful co-existence allows the Communists in capitalist lands to fight at the head of the masses for their liberation.

(4) The Chinese say that the Soviet Union is helping the national bourgeoisie to seize power. In the present phase of the struggle manoeuvring is necessary. But this does not mean that we lose sight of the ultimate objective. Military preparedness must be maintained; but disarmament is the ideal of Socialism. This is denied by the Chinese, who suggest a third way, the way of local wars. This way is impossible: it would lead to world war.

(5) The forces of capitalism must be met in conflict by the masses and the workers. We do not pretend that the parliamentary way to power is obligatory.

(6) The attitude of the Chinese leads to the isolation of China and the Communist countries. Thus, the Chinese refused to take

part in a Congress of Students; at a Congress of Women they refused to sit at the same table as bourgeois representatives; at the W.F.T.U. all the trade unions opposed the Chinese, who tried to prevent that organization from operating in the interests of peace.

(7) The cult of personality is a question on which the Chinese have reservations, although it is regarded as settled once and for all by all other Communist Parties.

(8) The Chinese attitude reinforces the position of the imperialists and allows them to sow dissension in the Communist camp.

(9) In sum, the Central Committee of the Soviet Party and the Central Committee of the Chinese Party are at variance. The Soviet Union is trying to take amicable steps to re-establish unity.

*

Before the Conference opened the delegates were given the score. They were told verbally that at the Preparatory Commission China had been supported by Albania, Vietnam, and Indonesia; that on the question of the cult of personality, the Chinese, the Albanians, and the Indonesians had refused to agree to the Soviet text; that on the question of fractional activities, the Chinese had been supported by the Japanese, North Korean, Indonesian, Vietnamese, and Australian Parties in their insistence that this matter must not be referred to in the declaration.

All this was clear and above board: the delegates had something serious to think about along the lines to which they were accustomed. They could forget the bad impression caused by Soviet lobbying and caucasing and address themselves, like conscientious comrades, to the real matter in hand – the reconciliation of Soviet and Chinese view-points, the re-establishment of unity in equality, and the publication of a policy document which would be binding for a unified movement.

But was this, after all, the real matter in hand? It began to look as though it was not. For almost at once the Russians circulated still another letter, this time of 127 pages, and dated 5 November, which, while purporting to answer the Chinese letter of 10 September, reposed itself not on ideological rectitude (though this, of course, was argued at great length), but on the superiority of the Soviet Union to the People's Republic of China.

Out of concern for unity, the main burden ran, the Soviet press has abstained from mentioning Soviet differences with the Chinese Party, regardless of the propaganda which has been carried on in the capitalist press and the indirect attacks on the Soviet Union in the Chinese press. But in fact, except for the Trotskyites, no group has ever abused the Soviet Party in the sort of terms used by the Chinese Party. The main preoccupation of the Chinese Party is to denigrate Khrushchev personally. They, the Chinese, must bear the responsibility for divergencies between the fraternal Parties.

The Chinese reproach Khrushchev personally for strengthening capitalism with his policy of peace. But the struggle for peace will be long, and the *peoples* of the capitalist lands are not our enemies. 'There is no need to burn the house down in order to kill fleas.'

The Chinese have criticized Khrushchev for his visit to the United States; but this visit enabled him to raise on high the flag of the struggle against imperialism.

The Chinese have singled out Khrushchev for attack; but all Khrushchev's policies are authorized by the Central Committee of the Soviet Party. His travels abroad have created difficulties for the imperialists. It is quite useless to try to disassociate Khrushchev from the Soviet Party.

The Chinese have cast aspersions on Soviet arms. But the Soviet army is powerful and can well ensure the defence of the Soviet Union and other fraternal countries, as was seen in the case of Hungary.

The Chinese criticize the Soviet Party on the question of the cult of personality. But Stalin liquidated a large part of the cadres of the Soviet army and hindered the development of the economy of the Soviet Union.

As for Albania, a number of Party leaders in Tirana have been imprisoned simply for supporting the Soviet Party.

The stage was set.

Chapter Twelve

THE FINAL BREACH:
MOSCOW 1960

IT was a curious occasion, and it is very much to be doubted whether the St George's Hall in the Kremlin will ever see its like again. For sheer inefficiency and time-wasting talk the Moscow Conference of November 1960 would be almost impossible to beat. It ran from 11 November to 25 November, drawing breath only on Sundays. Each morning session started at ten o'clock and went on until two; back again at four, and on until deep into the evening. But although a great many useless and wholly repetitive words were spoken and a great deal of time wasted listening to them, and although the dramatic highlights occupied only an insignificant amount of time, these when they came were very dramatic indeed. And for the rest we should be grateful for all that talk, because though much of it meant little or nothing to the assembled delegates, the inner ring of international Communist leaders who had heard it all before, it provides us with an immensely valuable insight into the preoccupations and the manner of thought of Communists all over the world.

One of the most striking aspects of the whole affair was the way in which the delegates, with the great Sino–Soviet issue clouding the sky throughout the conference, and, every so often, bursting into thunder and lightning, came with their set speeches and stuck to them. The fact that the Communist world was hanging in the balance, that the leaders of the two great Communist powers were actively trying to unseat each other, was not going to prevent the delegate from Guatemala, the delegate from Ceylon, the delegate from Iceland, holding forth about his own particular local problems as though no such thing as a struggle existed. They all had their say, and they all added careful phrases, sometimes conventional, sometimes inspired by warm feeling, about the great conflict. But one has the strong impression that if the Chinese, if the Albanians, had been more conciliatory and cool in tone and more subtle in argument there would have been far less condemnation of the Chinese and far more conventional appeals for the necessity of composing differences in the interests of unity. In a later chapter we shall consider the implications of some of these speeches for the future of Communism as a world movement; but for the moment we are concerned strictly with the development of the Sino–Soviet conflict as such.

Khrushchev, the host welcoming his guests, opened the proceedings with a conventional speech outlining the Soviet position, but indicating nothing of the storm that was to come. After procedural matters had been proposed by Pospelov, and settled, Suslov formally introduced his draft declaration which the delegates had already perused. He was at pains to emphasize that the Soviet Union had no use for imperialism, 'a ferocious bloodstained beast', and was very far from abandoning the revolutionary struggle. But there were ways and ways of taming the monster. The draft declaration he now tabled represented a great deal of work, and he thought the fact that it had been adopted as a basis for discussion was an achievement in itself. But divergencies still existed which had to be ironed out. He concluded by giving the delegates their cue: fractions must not be tolerated.

But soon the Russian line became apparent. The ball was set rolling, incongruously enough, by Mr Tim Buck of Canada, who sharply attacked the Chinese as 'left-wing deviationists' who had been ready to sacrifice their fraternal duties to the extent of risking an actual schism in the movement. The Chinese, he said, must practise self-criticism: their methods had provoked discord between the parties. They should have appealed to the Central Committees of fraternal parties to open a discussion; instead they had gone over the heads of the Central Committees by lobbying individual Communists. This behaviour was inadmissible. The arguments of the Chinese, moreover, did not conform to Marxist-Leninist principles.

And so it went on. In those first days speaker after speaker voiced his criticism of the Chinese, who were clearly taken aback by their unanimity, and particularly by attacks from Latin American and Middle Eastern Parties, persecuted and oppressed, whose only hope appeared to lie in violence, and to whom the militant Chinese attack might have been expected to appeal far more strongly than Soviet Fabianism. Then, on the 14th, came the turn of Teng Hsaio-ping. The delegates sat up.

The Chinese Party, he declared, adhered to the 1957 declaration, which had been very fruitful. But certain questions of principle remained to be settled and it was necessary to secure the agreement of all parties if the differences were to be removed by discussion.

But there was something wrong. What was particularly disturbing was the Soviet Party letter of 5 November which violently attacked the leadership of the Chinese Party and Mao Tsetung personally. This letter was much more important than the speech delivered on this platform on behalf of the Soviet Party – that is Khrushchev's opening speech.

By circulating this letter, and in other ways, the Soviet Party had abused its privileged position, which it owed to the fact that the conference was being held in Moscow. The Soviet Party had assembled arguments which misrepresented the Chinese position and were in fact lies.

It was an extraordinary moment. Here, in the heart of Moscow, in the great Kremlin hall still haunted by the ghost of Stalin who had dictated to every Party member throughout the globe with no fear of contradiction, the General Secretary of another great Party stood up and called Stalin's successor a liar to his face, not in private, but in front of comrades from every land. The roof did not fall.

Instead, Teng went on roughly and briskly to put the record straight. He was sick of hearing the Chinese position deliberately falsified and misrepresented. He began to state it again in the terms with which we are by now all too familiar.

But one of the most striking aspects of Teng's speech was the remarkable extent to which Communists have become prisoners of their own vocabulary. This stylized vocabulary, or jargon, quite clearly inhibits, or blunts, both understanding and expression as between Communists no less than as between Communists and non-Communists. Both the Chinese and Russians positively floundered in the efforts to define 'the present epoch' in Marxist terms – because both were using the same stereotypes to mean different things. Both accused each other of over-estimating the strength of imperialism and under-estimating the strength of the Socialist camp. But it became clear as Teng developed his argument that quite new phrases were needed (which neither Khrushchev nor Teng commanded) to express changing concepts (which neither, for lack of flexible vocabulary, could adequately define). It is therefore necessary to come to their rescue.

When the Chinese speak of the strength of imperialism, which they think the Russians over-estimate, they really mean (as Lenin mostly meant) its aggressive dynamic, which may drive it willy-nilly to war. But when the Russians speak of the strength of imperialism, which they think the Chinese under-estimate, they are thinking of its power of survival, its latent strength, in a changing world.

Again, when the Chinese speak of the strength of the Socialist camp, which they say the Russians under-estimate, they really mean its power, backed by Soviet nuclear arms, of delivering a death blow to an aggressive but declining imperialism, should it come to a show-down. But when the Russians speak of the strength of the Socialist camp, which they say the Chinese over-estimate, they are thinking of its power of survival in a changing world and its deterrent strength in face of imperialist belligerence.

These differences are at the root of the whole argument about war and peace. They are not understood by the Chinese at all. Whether they are understood by Khrushchev, who may be merely pretending not to understand in order to drive the Chinese to appear more and more warlike – and thus viewed with apprehension by the fraternal parties – it is impossible to tell.

Teng tried very hard to put his point of view across, but he muddled things badly. The Chinese had never said that world war or any war was inevitable, he said, only that it was all too probable, knowing the imperialists. And whether there was a war or not was entirely out of the hands of the Socialist camp: it depended on the imperialist chiefs-of-staff – a view which both we and Khrushchev like to think of as old-fashioned. All the Chinese said was that if the imperialists launched a nuclear war the choice would be between surrender and stubborn resistance: for a Communist that was no choice; he must resist. And he would win. So long as capitalism existed it would never be possible to say that there would be no more wars. As for local wars – in fact they happened. A Communist cannot declare himself vaguely against *all* local wars: there were 'just' local wars to be supported, and there were counter-revolutionary local wars to be fought. Further, it was untrue to say that local wars must lead to world war. He went on, with a nasty dig at Khrushchev: the Soviet Union itself with its threats of retaliatory action had stopped both Suez and Cuba from developing into major war; why was it so frightened?

He was all for trying to ensure world peace. There was a perfectly respectable world front for peace: it included the Socialist camp, with the Soviet Union at its head, the ex-colonial countries, which are neutral or allied, and the anti-imperialist elements of the capitalist countries themselves. But it did *not* include bourgeois politicians, and it could *not* be built on the 'goodwill' of imperialist statesmen. Arms were also needed. Talk about total disarmament was dishonest and misleading. So long as imperialism existed the army would remain an essential instrument of the State: a world without armies was a world without states. The policy of peaceful co-existence could only be *a part* of the foreign policy of socialist countries and Communist Parties.

He tried to define China's attitude towards national liberation in the backward countries. In liberated countries where the national bourgeois were in power it behoved all Communists to be very careful as to how they committed themselves. National bourgeois governments, even when the proletariat were allied with them on a given programme, should not be accepted blindly. Communists must have the courage to criticize them and show them up for what they are. Certainly support should be given to any alliance between the bourgeoisie and a part of the exploited classes in the first stage of the struggle against imperialism; but once the second stage began, when the workers, peasants, and intellectuals started their struggle against the bourgeois, it was another matter altogether: then there must be no tolerating the bourgeois nationalists.

India was a case in point. The Indian bourgeoisie put themselves beyond the pale at the end of 1959 on the occasion of the 'counter-revolution' in Tibet. What was now happening in India, with its deliberate frontier provocations, was a last desperate attempt of the bourgeoisie to play for time and postpone its inevitable overthrow at the hands of the people. Were Communists to help them survive? For long, Indian policy has been vacillating, and now Nehru had turned to the right and was manufacturing frontier disputes to postpone the day of reckoning with his own people. China, faced with a situation of this kind, was fully entitled to call on other Communist Parties for support against the 'Nehru clique', and particularly on the Communist Party of India. But instead of offering support the Soviet Party had taken the side of the Indian government, causing differences between fraternal parties and aggravating Sino–Indian relations.

Teng then became a schoolmaster. There was a correct formula, he said, to cover situations of this kind. It was best expressed as 'unity-struggle; struggle-unity'. 'Unity-struggle' meant struggling with those inclined to the right and uniting with those inclined to the left; 'struggle-unity' meant uniting with any of those who after being fought then turn to the left. In practice this meant pursuing a policy of friendship with Nehru while struggling against him, never forgetting that his internal difficulties were increasing day by day and that, as a result, his regime grew closer and closer to an imperialist regime.

This passage about India was a key passage. We shall have to discuss it later when we consider just how close to Leninism the world Communist movement, outside China, now stands. It was a classic statement of a Leninist attitude; and it did not go down at all well with many of the delegates, for whom it had an old-fashioned ring.

Teng then went on to question very sharply the 20th Congress thesis that Communism might be achieved without violence. Here he was at his most donnish: 'The validity of a thesis is not proved by constantly repeating the same formula.' The Russians had grossly over-estimated the role of parliaments in the transition to Socialism and, at the same time, denied the need (this was not strictly true) for preparing for two eventualities – peaceful and non-peaceful conquest of power. Peaceful action by

Communists was increasingly limited by the strength of entrenched 'bureaucracy'. So it was erroneous to suggest that the chances of gaining power by peaceful means were the greater. It was correct from a tactical point of view to insist on gaining power for peaceful means, but, Teng said in effect, we should not be taken in by our own slogans, and we must be ready for all eventualities. It was true enough to say that revolution could not be exported, but the Socialist camp must assist all peoples struggling for their liberation.

But it was when he came to the communes, the Great Leap Forward, and the sacred person of Mao Tse-tung that Teng's emotions got the upper hand and offered more than a glimpse at the profound hurt to Chinese pride inflicted by Soviet criticism of these sanctities.

The Chinese Party welcomed comradely criticism, he said; but for the Soviet comrades to describe the communes as a failure which had brought China to the brink of famine was fantastic; to accuse her, even in veiled language, of discrediting Communism in the eyes of the masses of Asia was nothing less than monstrous. He went into an almost lyrical panegyric of the wonderful achievements of the communes in raising the people of China up from the mud. And when he spoke of Mao, as the inspiration and the guiding light of China, even though removed now high above the day-to-day conduct of affairs, his words had a fervour almost mystical, so that his eulogy was far removed in tone from the fulsome but conventional flattery with which the Russian leaders had once spoken of Stalin.

'The Soviet Party has tried to discredit the Chinese Party by attributing to it theses which it has never proclaimed. . . . The Chinese Party adapts the universal truth of Marxist-Leninism to the concrete conditions of China. We adapt Marxism to China; we do not sinify Marxism. . . . Nobody will ever succeed in denigrating Mao Tse-tung. It is Mao who united our party and people. It is he who showed us the way.'

Teng then returned to earth. He was determined to settle the charge of fractionalism brought against the Chinese Party once and for all. And it soon became clear that what the Chinese were really doing was trying to establish a pattern of relationships between the various parties which might one day, when the

Chinese Party was relatively stronger, transfer the leadership of the world Communist movement to Pekin. This and this alone could account for the extreme insistence of Teng and other Chinese speakers on a reassertion of the leading role of the Soviet Party at the very moment when they were violently attacking it. Khrushchev, and other speakers following his lead, were anxious to drop the formal Soviet title to leadership. The Chinese Party, even as they disputed with Moscow, did their level best to pin it back.

There had to be a leading party, and the leading party was the Soviet Party. Nevertheless there must be complete equality between countries. Criticism was not incompatible with unity. Everything that Lenin had said about fractionalism applied only to the political line of individual parties, not to inter-party relationships between countries. 'In relations between Parties there is no reason to demand that the minority should submit to the majority, for between parties there are no superiors and inferiors: each party is independent. ... The Soviet Party accuses us of fractionalism for disputing certain resolutions passed by its own Congresses. But it is only the Soviet Party which can be bound by its own Congresses. In trying to bind others it is the Soviet Party which has offended against inter-party discipline. For how can there be equality between fraternal parties if everything the Soviet Party decides at its own Congresses is binding on the rest? Or must we admit a new concept – "father" Parties and "son" Parties? The purpose behind the condemnation in the draft resolution of the activities of fractions and groups is intended to place a bomb under the Chinese Party, and nothing else at all. We shall not yield!' Further, if the Chinese Party is guilty of fractionalism in seeking to disseminate its own views, then Lenin himself was a fractionalist. By splitting the Social Democratic Party into Bolsheviks and Mensheviks, Lenin had formed what was at first a minority fraction in order to win for himself an ultimate majority. The Chinese had an equal right to form a fraction of this kind. And history would tell whether or not the Chinese, in a minority, were wrong.

This was the real declaration of war. In a world-wide movement which so far had depended on iron discipline and absolute unity, for decades imposed by Moscow, and buttressed by sacred writings, the Chinese Party was announcing its right to break ranks, to develop its own line, to proselytize and intrigue in its favour, to turn a minority into a majority, and, ultimately, when that majority was won, to succeed Moscow as the 'leading party'.

After that the rest of Teng's speech was anti-climax. This was not a family quarrel. It was notice of that most dreaded, most anathematized thing in the Communist movement – a split; and although both main parties concerned might show themselves ready to conceal the split from the outside world, for reasons of expediency, it was no longer a question – on this November day in 1960 – of whether a split might come: the split was proclaimed by the Secretary-General of the Chinese Communist Party, speaking with the blessing of Mao.

It was a traumatic moment. But the conference continued for the time being as though nothing had happened to shake the foundations of the movement. Criticism of the Chinese attitude became much sharper. Mr Bikdash, the Syrian Communist leader, put the question most clearly. He accused the Chinese of putting nationalist interests above international ones. He said the Chinese comrades were impossible: if any one offered the least breath of criticism they took it as a declaration of war. He poured scorn on Teng's claims for the communes. The Chinese Party had imposed on the Chinese people a gigantic burden of work, which was beyond human strength, 'just like Nasser in the United Arab Republic'. But the communes had only one purpose: to reject the experience of the Soviet Union. It was impossible to believe in the sincerity of the Chinese Party in reaffirming the leading role of the Soviet Party when it was at the same time covering the Soviet Party with abuse. The Chinese Party was attempting to detach the other parties from the Soviet Party. He went on to ask: 'Can the Chinese Party have any place in the ranks of the Communist movement after such behaviour?'

Nobody followed this line. It was as though no other delegate could bring himself publicly to echo this logical conclusion. Teng had spoken on the 14th. All through the 15th there was an air of unreality. Then, on the 16th, there came release. It came in the shape of a speech by Enver Hoxha of Albania, who had already allied himself intimately with the Chinese in their quarrel with Russia, and was not repulsed by them. Later, as we know, when the dispute came half out into the open in the autumn of 1961, Albania became the code-word for China in all Soviet attacks. And speeches allegedly written by Enver Hoxha were couched in Chinese imagery. What started all this was Hoxha's wild and violent onslaught on Khrushchev personally.

Imperialism, he started off, was on the decline, but it had not changed its nature and it was preparing for war. Understanding this, the Albanian people worked with a rifle in one hand and a pick in the other. Anybody who did not see that imperialism was preparing war was blind. Those who saw it, but tried to conceal it, were worse than blind, they were traitors. . . .

The Chinese and the Albanian Communists were naturally in favour of peaceful co-existence, which presupposed an intensification of the class-struggle for the progressive liquidation of imperialism. But Khrushchev had muddled Lenin's teachings in order to suit his own purposes. No Communist Party had yet been able to seize power without violence. . . .

He went on to attack the Soviet pressurizing tactics at Bucarest. The Bucarest meeting had been hastily prepared on Soviet initiative and the Chinese Party had been arraigned in front of other parties on the basis of Soviet allegations alone. 'Did Khrushchev and other Soviet leaders have such little confidence in their cause that they found it necessary to resort to such underhand trickery?'

He went on to describe the particular pressures, which, he alleged, had been brought by the Russians against the Albanians to influence them against their own party leadership and 'force them to choose between the 200 million Russians and the 650 million Chinese'. Khrushchev, he said, had boasted to Teng Hsaio-ping: 'We shall treat Albania as we treated Yugoslavia', and he had carried out that threat. Albania's only crime had been to be small, poor, and courageous in its views. She had suffered earthquakes and floods, a drought lasting 120 days and the threat of famine. She had only fifteen days' supply of grain in store. The Russians had deliberately exploited this situation, offering a fraction of what they had promised, and that far too late. 'The Soviet rats had been able to feed while the Albanian people were starving. And for the little they gave they demanded payment in gold.'

He then moved in, as was to be expected, into a violent tirade against Tito and Khrushchev's wooing of him. Documents, he said, were being dug out to condemn Stalin, but the greatest care was being taken to conceal any documents that might incriminate Tito. This was characteristic. Stalin had been a world-famous figure and the true continuer of Lenin's cause. Tito was an imperialist of the deepest dye, and all the talk of trying to win him back into the Socialist camp was little short of criminal. To have approached him, as Khrushchev approached him in 1955, had been an error of the crassest kind. The Cominform resolution, expelling Yugoslavia, had been perfectly correct. Why had Khrushchev suddenly started off on a new line without the least warning? It had been nothing less than a bombshell, and the Albanians had at once registered a protest. But, under cover of this new development the 'Titoist' group in the Albanian Party had started a witch-hunt against him, Hoxha, and his colleagues and done their best to liquidate them. The next thing was that Tito was hard at work coordinating the counter-revolution in Hungary, and Khrushchev was reposing more confidence in him than in the Albanians. He had nothing but contempt for the way the Russians had treated Stalin's memory and for the whole drift of their post-Stalin policy.

Enver Hoxha's speech, as already observed, not only shook the delegates to the core, it also acted as a release. Those who were unhappy and inhibited when it came to denouncing China, presided over by Mao, the great father-figure, far-seeing and wise, need have no such inhibitions about the leader of a tiny Balkan state who had achieved his position not by virtue of Marxist conviction, but as a mountain bandit with a Western education who had exploited the appeal of Communism to further the interests of his own family dynasty, operating with traditional violence and intrigue for purely personal ends.

When Gomulka of Poland got up to speak he was able to exploit the new mood. He did not wish to wound the Chinese comrades, he said, by stigmatizing them as dogmatists, revisionists, fractionalists, sectarians, Trotskyites, schismatics – but what else were they to be called? As for the Albanians, Enver Hoxha had made 'a disgusting, shameful, gangsterish, irresponsible attack on Khrushchev and the Soviet Party'. Proletarian internationalism should be able to prohibit any individual, any party, from calumniating the leaders of other parties while, at the same time, cynically and hypocritically, affirming that they stood at the head of the Socialist movement. In Albania portraits of Khrushchev had been taken down and replaced by those of Stalin. Hoxha would not have been able to behave like this when Stalin was alive!

This was the background to Khrushchev's attack on Albania at the 22nd Congress of the Soviet Party in October 1961. After that, for a year, all Soviet attacks on China were directed ostensibly at Albania. The interesting thing is that neither at the Moscow meeting in 1960, immediately after Hoxha's speech, nor at any time afterwards were the Chinese to disassociate themselves from the Albanians. When, at Moscow, Teng spoke again (on 24 November) in reply to Khrushchev's attack, he did not, as many expected he would do, take the opportunity to suggest that, while China sympathized with the Albanian position, she deplored the use of such language. On the contrary, it was Gomulka he attacked. Hoxha, he said, had made charges against the Soviet Union's conduct in state and party relations with Albania; but good relations could be restored. On the other hand, 'Gomulka had insulted Albania by his filthy attack', and this had astonished the Chinese, who regarded it as harmful to the unity of the movement. . . . As for Khrushchev himself, a large part of his speech had been directed against Mao without mentioning him directly. 'Khrushchev had evidently been talking without knowing what he was saying, as he did all too frequently.'

This was, in effect, the Chinese last word. They had come in fighting, and they went out fighting. But they were forced to give way. 'We shall not yield!' Teng had exclaimed over the matter of fractionalism; but in the end there was a compromise: the actual word 'fractionalism' was excluded from the famous Moscow Declaration. Faced as the Chinese were by the, to them, unexpected display of solidarity of the fraternal parties behind Khrushchev, there was nothing to do but yield, in the interests of apparent unity, or withdraw from the conference and proclaim that Pekin henceforward was the real, the spiritual headquarters of the Communist movement. This they were not ready to do. Quite apart from the fact that the Chinese still desperately needed material help from the Soviet Union, to have precipitated an open breach at this time would have been a strategic error of the grossest kind. They and they alone would have had to bear the responsibility of splitting the Communist movement in two. Apart from the Albanian, the Burmese, the Malayan and, astonishingly, the Australian Parties, they would have been quite alone.

Further, the rank and file of Communists everywhere were quite unprepared. It has to be remembered that the great debates at Bucarest and Moscow took place behind closed doors. Only the higher leadership of the eighty-one parties knew what really went on. There was nothing in either the Chinese or the Soviet press to inform the millions of the faithful of the true state of affairs. As far as publicity was concerned, Khrushchev was having things all his own way with his highly popular policy of nuclear restraint and rapprochement with the imperialists. China's only hope was that as the ideological grounds for the dispute became better known the rank-and-file membership would start asking questions. They were doing so already in some of those countries where the only hope for Communism seemed to lie through violence. That was what was meant by certain of the Latin American delegates when they said that Chinese activity was already producing fissions in their own parties. When the Chinese decided to sign the Declaration they did so only on the firm understanding that there should be another full-dress meeting of all the parties within two years. By that time, it is clear, they hoped that many of the fraternal parties would have got over the first shock of the very idea of the conflict and would be in a mood to ask more reasonably what it was really about, instead of rallying instinctively round the traditional Muscovite banner. But it was no longer a question of whether or not things would come to a schism: the schism existed. Khrushchev and Mao were at each other's throats, and so they remained.

*

Meanwhile the fraternal parties took up the fight. All the delegates to Moscow reported back to their flocks, but a year was to
go by before what some of them had said was given to a wider
public. Then the French, the Italians, and the Belgians all published their own accounts which confirmed, and sometimes
added to, what had already become known. Thorez, indeed, in
November 1961, gave the most clear and concise account then
extant of the fundamental ideological differences while, at the
same time, bitterly reproaching the Chinese for importing into
what should have been an ideological discussion problems of
Sino–Soviet State relations, which had nothing to do with
Communism. He also sought to show that the dispute was not
simply a matter of ideological niceties, but a fundamental cleavage within the Movement:

... We have now acquired the certitude that it is not a matter of
disagreements limited to two or three points of the Declaration proposed to this Conference, but of an entire line opposed to the international Communist movement.

We have at the same time confirmation that it is not a matter of
divergencies between the Chinese Communist Party and the Communist Party of the Soviet Union, but of a profound disagreement of
the Chinese comrades with the whole international Communist
movement. . . .[1]

The Belgian account was more emotional. Having paraphrased
Teng's speech at Moscow, with particular reference to the
Chinese thesis that 'We must stop referring to the 20th Congress
of the Soviet Communist Party as if its teachings were valid for
the entire world Communist movement . . . ever since the 20th
Congress that Party has led the majority of the Communist
Parties along the road of surrender to the imperialists', it went
on to declare that in the Chinese standpoint

... there is a blanket denial of the validity and the usefulness of the
criticism of the cult of personality; there is anger at the idea that it is
possible and useful to prevent the start of a third world war; there is
doubt as to the political advantage to be gained by upgrading the
different paths to Socialism; there is scorn for the 'utopian' belief in
the theory of bloodless ways for the working class to rise to power in
some countries, and under given conditions. . . .[2]

Chapter Thirteen

THE STRUGGLE FOR ASCENDANCY

THE purpose of this narrative so far has been to establish the genesis of the dispute between Moscow and Pekin and to demonstrate its increasing bitterness and range first by reading what could be read (what, indeed, was intended to be read by the fraternal parties) between the lines in the Soviet and Chinese press, then by correlating what could be read with visible Soviet and Chinese actions, then by summarizing the proceedings of the two formal meetings in Bucarest and Moscow.

The main point that emerges from this narrative is that in the second half of 1960 the dispute reached a major climax amounting to nothing less than a split, visible to all within the Communist movement, but still concealed from the outer world. What happened after that was to be in no sense an addition to what had gone before – both sides had presented their cases by the end of the Moscow meeting and thereafter were to rest on them – but, rather, a process of elaborate and intricate manoeuvring for advantage within the Communist camp. And this went on for another two years, until December 1962, when first the Russians, then the Chinese, for the first time admitted to the outside world the existence of a split and thereafter proceeded to carry on the debate partly in public, a phase which reached a new climax in March 1963 when the Chinese claimed for themselves, first in the *People's Daily*, then in an immense statement of their position in the *Red Flag*, that they and not the Russians were the true heirs of Lenin and Marx. They rubbed the lesson home by paraphrasing the most evocative words in the Communist scriptures, and applying them to Pekin, seen as the true headquarters of world Communism.

The opening words of the Communist Manifesto of 1848, which every Communist has by heart, are: 'A spectre is haunting Europe – the spectre of Communism.'

The Chinese variant, first published in the *People's Daily* of 1 March 1963, ran:

A spectre is haunting the world – the spectre of genuine Marxist-Leninism, and it threatens you. You have no faith in the people, and the people have no faith in you. You are divorced from the masses. That is why you fear the truth.

'You', of course, was Khrushchev, who was thus equated with the enemy of the Communist Manifesto, which went on: 'All the powers of old Europe have entered into a holy alliance to exorcise this spectre: Pope and Tsar, Metternich and Guizot, French Radicals and German police-spies.'

Pekin's deliberate transplantation of the spectre image in order to put Khrushchev on a level with the reactionaries of 1848 was the most decisive blow he had struck. It was a formal declaration of war. It was a summons to all who held to the true faith to ally themselves under the banner of Mao Tse-tung to throw down the Russian renegades.

There is no need in this study to pursue the detail of the manoeuvres on both sides between the 1960 formalization of the conflict and the publication of its existence to the world, two years later. There were a few high points.

After the publication of the Moscow Declaration of 1960 there was a great show of solidarity. Pekin's price for signing it had been an assurance that Soviet technicians would be allowed to return. This happened. And in February 1961 a Soviet economic mission arrived in Pekin. The 11th anniversary of the Sino–Soviet Pact was celebrated with considerable ostentation. But nothing much was done. And the Soviet economic mission was headed only by a deputy Minister from the Ministry of Foreign Trade.

Nothing much was said, either. For a time both the Soviet and the Chinese Press went very quietly, and little was openly said to exacerbate a situation which was already out of control. Soviet Communist functionaries of both high and low degree maintained a complete silence about the quarrel: it was a figment of a disordered imagination, part of the deliberate campaign of calumny engendered by the cold war they would say – if, indeed, they said anything at all. And that was that.

Behind the scenes, however, there was continuing activity. Both sides circulated letters among the fraternal parties justifying their own points of view, and the Russians, for good measure, piled on further details about Chinese anti-Soviet subversion. While the Chinese were content in public to show that their attitude had not changed by, for example, writing about President Kennedy in terms of total obloquy at a time when Khrushchev was making his first conciliatory approaches to Eisenhower's successor – approaches which turned sour in the course of the fatal Vienna meeting in June 1961 – the Russians were staging a number of fairly provocative demonstrations. Thus, in July, they signed a treaty of alliance with North Korea, which bound the Soviet Union more closely to the Koreans than to the Chinese; and a week later the Yugoslav Foreign Minister, Popovic, was received with acclaim in Moscow when he went to prepare the way for a new rapprochement between Khrushchev and the arch-revisionist, the 'Trojan Horse of the imperialists'. In the same month there was a marked lack of Soviet participation at the celebration of the fortieth anniversary of the Chinese Communist Party: none of the higher Soviet leadership attended; there was no personal message from Khrushchev to Mao; routine goodwill messages from most of the fraternal parties were cool in tone.

Then, at the end of the month, Moscow came out with the draft of a new programme for the Soviet Communist Party.

This programme had to come, Chinese or no Chinese. It was only the third in the history of the Bolshevik Party, and it was overdue. The first Party programme had been promulgated in 1903, when the Tsar was very firmly on the throne: it called for the overthrow of the Tsarist autocracy, of the 'bourgeois-landlord' system, and the establishment of the dictatorship of the proletariat. The second followed in 1919, when the first programme had been fulfilled, less by Lenin and his Bolsheviks than by less ruthless and disciplined and more human and expansive revolutionary parties, which were swiftly destroyed by Lenin, when he had climbed to power on their backs. It called for the building of a Socialist society in the Soviet Union. This task, also, as Moscow saw it in 1961, had been fulfilled.

What next? The main task outlined in the new Party programme was the building of Communism, as distinct from Socialism, in the Soviet Union and the further advance of the Socialist revolution throughout the world.

The gigantic revolutionary exploits of the Soviet people have roused and inspired the masses in all countries and all continents. A mighty, unifying thunderstorm, marking the springtime of mankind, is raging all over the earth. The Socialist revolution in European and Asian countries has resulted in the establishment of a world Socialist system. A powerful wave of national liberation revolutions is sweeping away the colonial system of imperialism.

One third of mankind is building a new life under the banner of scientific Communism. The first contingents of the working class to shake off obsolete oppression are facilitating victory for fresh contingents of their class brothers. The Socialist world is expanding; the capitalist world is shrinking. Socialism will inevitably succeed capitalism everywhere. Such is the objective law of social development.

That was the mood. And there was a great deal about the Western world, above all America, which, to the casual eye, might have seemed pleasing to Pekin. But Pekin did not rejoice.

In this immense and jubilant document, with its sweeping, generalized claims for the victorious advance of Socialism, there is a marked neglect of China, the great partner, who, when all was said, accounted for rather more than one half of the 'third of mankind building a new life under the banner of Socialism'. There was a great deal about national liberation movements, and Khrushchev's policy of aid to the newly independent countries, whether 'bourgeois nationalist' or not, was heavily underlined. There was a great deal of thunder about the doom of capitalism and the advance of what the Russians like to call Socialism. But when it came to the matter of practical advice as to how this advance was to be contrived, as to how the glorious Soviet Union in its embattled might might assist its weaker, poorer, persecuted brethren – when it came to this, which should have been the prime object of any new Soviet Party programme, there was nothing. Nor was there the least expression of solicitude or concern for the struggles of those Socialist countries which, having achieved their own revolutions (for example China) or having had their revolutions thrust upon them by Soviet troops (that is all the Communist countries of Europe except Yugoslavia), were for one reason or another suffering hard times – either because like China they were desperately poor to begin with, or because like Czechoslovakia they had been plundered by Stalin. Instead, page after page, section after section of this egregious document, which reads like a prospectus of the American way of life compiled before the great depression, is devoted to the glorification of the material progress of the Soviet Union and to shame-making bragging (the dated word best describes the dated approach) to the effect that in twenty years time the Soviet Union would be the most prosperous country in the world, leaving America behind. The rest of the Socialist camp might not have existed. The Moscow comrades, intoxicated by the prospect of free bread for all, did not even bother to pay lip-service to the idea that it might be their duty to help their less privileged comrades. The new Party programme could be summed up as the White Man's hymn of praise to himself. About the White Man's burden there was nothing. All it needed was an Elgar to set it to music.

The Russian comrades, who compiled this masterpiece, may be forgiven. Until quite recently there had been still so many Russians without enough bread that free bread had a symbolic significance – free doctors too and social services for the peasants, including holidays with pay, pensions, and sickness benefits; free secondary education for all. All the things we had been led to believe for so long that the Russians already had. . . .

But the aspect of the Party programme which offended the Chinese above all was the deliberate emphasis throughout on economic advance, as opposed to political action, as the true road to the Communist millennium.

I have already referred to Khrushchev's equation of Communism with abundance. It may be retorted that Communism has always been about abundance, and this in a sense is true. But not in Khrushchev's sense. In the whole of the writings of Marx and Lenin there is nothing to indicate that in their view the achievement of a Communist society was dependent on the accumulation of material wealth (by whom?) on such a scale that as a result of sheer abundance there would be as much of everything as every one could conceivably demand. Lenin saw the Communist society as the society in which, exploitation of man by man being forbidden, all would share and share alike in good times and in bad, in stringency or abundance, all for each and each for all. Of course he aimed at abundance, but he never intended that Communism should wait for its coming; on the contrary, a society organized on Communist lines was the very society to create abundance most certainly and swiftly.

It was Stalin who, in 1931, denounced all ideas of egalitarianism as petit-bourgeois heresies, and presented with the air of a great inventor the notion that differentials and material incentives were the greatest stimulus to hard work and increased productivity. It was the Stalin Constitution of 1937, still in force, which defined *Socialism* as meaning 'from each according to his ability; to each according to his work' (a fairly classic description of the American way of life – with the important proviso that able individuals were not allowed to exploit the labour of less able individuals for their own profit – a privilege reserved for the State); *Communism* as meaning 'from each according to his ability; to each according to his needs'. But even Stalin did not lay it down that a certain level of abundance had to be reached before this formula became operative.

That was left to Khrushchev. And by equating Communism with abundance he was in effect saying this: he was saying that it is impossible for a Communist society to create abundance. Only when abundance has been created by other means (in the case of the Soviet Union by what Stalin and Khrushchev call Socialism, what others call State capitalism) can Communism be achieved. It is nice to know that when the national wealth of the Soviet Union has reached a certain stage (higher than the national wealth of the United States today, Khrushchev says) the national cake is going to be divided up 'to each according to his needs'. But what this has to do with Communism as a dynamic system it is very hard to see. And it can hold the very minimum of interest for the oppressed toilers of a hundred lands existing on starvation rations. The fact that Khrushchev's claims are not true, that the Soviet Union herself still has a very long way to go before she can begin to compare in material prosperity with the advanced countries of the West, is no real comfort for these, who in any case do not know that the claims are not true: they see the *sputniks* circling the globe and assume that the Russians all live well – though why they should assume this when they know that America also contrives to combine advanced spacemanship with five million unemployed it is again hard to see.

Be that as it may, to the Chinese the Soviet Party programme conveyed, as it was intended to convey, a simple and unequivocal message: We are advanced; you are backward. We are rich; you are poor. We have enough to eat; you have not. We shall soon have more than any other country in the world; you will not. We have the hydrogen bomb; you have not. Anyone who doubts this on the grounds that vulgarity of this kind is inconceivable in this day and age should read a selection of Khrushchev's speeches, to say nothing of the Party programme itself. The sort of vulgarity we associate with ruling circles in England at the turn of the century is not peculiar to a single class, as a glance at the very rich of the United States would show us. The 'new class' of the Soviet Union, peasants and workers by birth, or the children of peasants and workers, already have their diamonds; they will soon have their 'Souls'.

But not yet the Chinese.

After the Party programme came the 22nd Party Congress in October, with Khrushchev's open attack on Albania, the casting of Stalin's body out of Lenin's tomb, and Chou En-lai's protest and pointed return to Pekin. What followed was an intensification of the struggle for power and influence within the Communist world. For a time it looked as though those men in China (among them, reputedly, Chou En-lai himself) who did not want to push the quarrel to the bitter end had gained in authority and influence. But if these had any hope that Khrushchev would seize the opportunity to make conciliatory gestures, they were wrong. Instead, he sought in many ways to press his advantage and to stress his hostility to Chinese pretensions; the chief among these was the promise to India to supply her with jet fighters.

By the summer of 1962 Pekin had started fighting back, this

time laying great emphasis on the iniquities of the 'economic heresy', which, in the tradition of Bernstein, advocates the achievement of Communism through economic progress and 'evolutionary' means rather than by direct political action – the thesis of the new Party programme. When, in September, Khrushchev reopened negotiations with Tito by sending Brezhnev, the nominal President of the Soviet Union, on a state visit to Belgrade, Chinese vituperation exceeded itself. Even before that Pekin had refused to join with Moscow in the development of a Communist Common Market. Now the air was filled with broadcasts of offensive leading articles from the Chinese press, translated into Russian and beamed to the Soviet Union. There were fresh denunciations of all ideas of an agreement between the Soviet Union and the United States to limit the spread of atomic weapons – talk of such an agreement could only be 'blackmail' directed against China and other Socialist lands. Towards the end of September the Chinese turned a plenary meeting of their Communist Party Central Committee into an occasion for the glorification of violent revolutionary action. At the same time a scarcely covert attack on Moscow referred to 'scheming activities . . . intrusion, provocation, and subversion within a State or a Party' – an attack which appeared to confirm earlier rumours that in the early summer there had been a serious diplomatic incident involving the discovery of active underground subversion in China conducted by Soviet agents.

Then all was overshadowed, in October, by the extraordinary episode of Khrushchev's advance into Cuba and his retreat from what appeared to be the very brink of nuclear war under direct pressure from the American president. This is not the place to speculate on the reasons which induced Khrushchev to install his rockets in Cuba (the room for argument here is unlimited; nobody *knows*), or to elaborate on his reasons for taking them away, which, basically, were obvious enough. The Cuban episode concerns us here only because of its effect on Pekin and the world Communist movement as a whole.

This was shattering. It gave the Chinese a supreme opportunity; but they were quite unable to exploit that opportunity because their own action in invading India gave them no room for intelligent manoeuvre. There seems little doubt that, apart from more obvious reasons, the Indian invasion had been undertaken as an essay in forcing tactics vis-à-vis Moscow. The promise of Soviet fighters to India was not only an affront to Pekin; it was a positive danger. Would Khrushchev dare implement that promise if China and India were at war with each other? If he showed that he dared, then this would be a final exposure of Muscovite perfidy towards the Socialist camp. If he did not dare, then his holding back would be an open humiliation. In the event, Khrushchev so managed to confuse the issue by postponements and delays and the spreading of inspired stories now to the effect that the M.I.G.s would be forthcoming, now to the effect that they would not, that the issue was never allowed to crystallize out. And the situation that arose, as seen by the fraternal parties, was that although Khrushchev had shown himself in Cuba a most unreliable leader, thus confirming Chinese charges, the Chinese in India had shown themselves to be reckless, belligerent, and highly nationalistic, thus confirming Soviet charges. It was an unhappy situation for the comrades; and long after the event it remained unresolved.

Which side came best out of it? We do not know. Khrushchev himself does not know. The fraternal parties themselves have not yet made up their minds.

The immediate reaction of the Chinese was to call the Cuban retreat another Munich. Khrushchev had his own story ready. It was plausible enough, but nobody believed it. The United States had been threatening Cuba with invasion. He had gone to the help of Castro and, by stationing nuclear rockets on the island, shown the Americans what would happen if they tried to invade. After a good deal of bluster, after instituting a blockade and threatening to sink any Soviet ship which tried to run it, President Kennedy had seen reason and solemnly pledged his word that there would be no invasion. This being so, he, Khrushchev, had been pleased to withdraw his rockets: they were no longer needed in Cuba, they had achieved their purpose there; they had saved this corner of the Western hemisphere for Communism; he could put them to better use elsewhere. And, as though deliberately echoing his praise of Eisenhower which had so incensed the Chinese in 1959, he paid tribute to the statesmanlike wisdom of President Kennedy, together with his own: between them the American President and the First Secretary of the Communist Party and Prime Minister of the Soviet Union had saved the peace of the world. Soon afterwards, on the forty-fifth anniversary of Lenin's revolution, he was saying that although the Soviet Union and the United States did not like each other 'they would probably have to embrace'.

Indeed, the whole Cuban affair as presented by Khrushchev was made to appear as a copy-book exercise to justify his thesis that, in this modern age, with the 'imperialists' themselves sobered by the power of the Socialist camp and the fear of nuclear annihilation, Communism could indeed conquer without war. It might have been designed for that purpose. But the Communist Parties of the world did not think so. Why, they asked, did Khrushchev go into Cuba with rockets at all if all he could do next was to back down? Was he, after all, a fit leader for the movement? They remembered that far from proclaiming the presence of the rockets in a gesture of defiance, at first the official Soviet spokesman (but never Khrushchev himself) had denied their very existence – and made them echo that denial.

Meanwhile the Chinese continued to make propaganda. They urged Castro to stand by his five points – for example evacuation by the U.S.A. of the Guantanamo base, retention of the Soviet bombers. They recalled their ambassadors from a number of East European states. They accused the 'revisionists' of acting as 'propagandists, political agents, and stooges of imperialism'. They exalted the Cuban revolution into one of the great climacterics of history, third only to the Soviet and Chinese revolutions. They flatly contradicted Khrushchev's claim to have saved the world from war. On the contrary, said the *People's Daily*, the retreat from Cuba has made war only more likely. For a Communist to bow before the imperialists, even to sue for peace with them, at the expense of 'the revolutionary people' is to encourage them in their aggressiveness and belligerence and thus make nuclear war more likely. In that same article there was a passionate appeal to Communists everywhere to put principle before expediency. Was world peace to be secured by 'the mass struggle of the peoples' or by relying on the benevolence, the promises, the reason of men like President Kennedy? The implication was that if the latter course was chosen, then there was no point at all in talking any more about the revolutionary struggle.

That was in November. In the first week of December Tito paid his return state visit to the Soviet Union, and for the first time since 1948 Party relations between Moscow and Belgrade were resumed. In the same week at the Congress of the Italian Communist Party Signor Togliatti made a major speech indirectly attacking Chinese policies in the presence of the Chinese delegate, and Signor Pajetta had the historic privilege of being the first Communist publicly to attack the Chinese by name: 'When we mean China we have no need to say Albania.' Almost at once his example was followed by speakers at the Czechoslovak Congress. The Chinese reacted quickly. Khrushchev has accused us, said the *People's Daily*, of adventurism; but what was the affair of rockets for Cuba but sheer irresponsible adventurism? And what was the subsequent withdrawal of those rockets but gross capitulation? A new word had been added to the traditional vocabulary of Communist invective.

In January 1963 came the Congress of the East German Party when the Chinese delegate, protesting against the Soviet rapprochement with Tito (there were representatives of ths Yugoslav Party at both the Rome and the Berlin Congresses), was shouted down. The stage was set for the thunderous exchange of newspaper polemics which reached their climax in the *Red Flag* article of 3 March. This was the article referred to earlier in which Pekin evoked the opening words of the Communist Manifesto of 1848, equating Khrushchev by implication with the reactionary autocrats of that day: 'A spectre is haunting the world – the spectre of genuine Marxist-Leninism, and it threatens you. . . .'

Immediately before the appearance of that article the Chinese press had published in translation a number of the more studied Soviet attacks on Chinese policy. Now *Red Flag* challenged Moscow to reciprocate, to publish the Chinese articles in the Soviet press, so that the people might judge which side was in the right. It taunted Khrushchev with being afraid of telling his people the truth, of letting them see for themselves what the Chinese had to say. Khrushchev was unmoved and did not respond. He was indeed afraid of telling his people the truth, but not for the reasons imagined by the Chinese. He had no fears that the Soviet people might be subverted, might suddenly decide that Mao's ideology was correct and Khrushchev's ideology false. They were not interested in Mao's ideology, or Khrushchev's either, as he knew very well. The reason why Khrushchev did not accept the Chinese challenge and publish their articles was because he did not wish to inflame popular national feeling against the Chinese. Should he ever wish to do so, the surest way would be for him to publish selected extracts from those articles – they are too long for even *Pravda* to print in full.

The background to this climactic phase of press polemics was a savage manoeuvring for position between Moscow and Pekin vis-à-vis the fraternal parties. With the *Red Flag* article Mao issued a formal challenge for the leadership of the Communist world: what had been implicit since Teng's declaration on fractionalism at the Moscow meeting in 1960, a declaration made to a strictly limited audience behind closed doors, was now made explicit and public. Mao was not merely appealing to the leaders of the fraternal parties; he was appealing to the rank and file, if necessary over the heads of the leaders. He was inviting every Communist who could read to decide the case on its merits for himself. And he wanted, was demanding, another full-scale conference of all the parties, a repetition of the 1960 Moscow Conference, to thresh out the issue once more. Khrushchev, on the other hand, wished at all costs to postpone such a meeting. He urged instead a restricted meeting between Chinese and Russians in an attempt to compose matters between them: meanwhile public polemics, which only gave comfort to the enemy and demoralized the fraternal parties, should cease. He took this line because, after Cuba, he no longer felt confident that he could swing the vast majority of the fraternal parties into line behind him, as he had been able to swing them into line in 1960. Mao, for his part, was sure that he had made important converts.

Chapter Fourteen

THE SHATTERED MONOLITH

I

IT is unnecessary to summarize the *Red Flag* article. We have already been over nearly all the ground it covered. Far more interesting was the Chinese reply to Signor Togliatti in the *People's Daily* of 31 December 1962 and the Soviet reply in *Pravda* on 6 January 1963.

Signor Togliatti's article was in effect no more than a restatement of the speech made by Signor Longo at the Moscow Conference in November 1960. This was a most remarkable performance because it highlighted the ideological differences between the pro-Chinese and the pro-Soviet factions more sharply than anything Khrushchev himself said. Indeed it took Khrushchev's thought to its logical conclusion. It went farther than the Russians themselves were prepared to go, and yet it was never contradicted by the Russians, or by any of their supporters.

What Signor Longo did, in effect, was to proclaim the death-knell of the Communist movement as hitherto understood. For the main burden of his speech, spelt out in further detail by Togliatti two years later, was to the effect that the Italian Communist Party was not interested in the proving of theories or the propounding of dogma but, exclusively, in achieving a better life for the masses. It did not mind how this was done; it did not pick and choose the people and organizations it worked with, so long as the goal was reached. More than this, it did not look forward to the victory of Communism as such, but, rather, to the creation, with the help of all men of good will, wherever they might be found, of a new kind of international society, no matter what it might be called.

This, of course, was a quintessential exposition of the 're-formist' heresy, which Lenin had fought all his life to kill. It came in the course of a speech in which Longo put more clearly than anybody else what so many of the fraternal parties, above all in Europe, were thinking about the Chinese doctrine that Communists must still reckon with the possibility of war, and be prepared to meet it without flinching.

Any idea of this kind would sap all impulse and vigour of action from the masses. The masses cannot be made to struggle for objectives which we ourselves declare to be unrealizable [that is revolution through war]. On the other hand, it must be remembered that without precise and energetic action on our part to mobilize the people against imperialist war, the way would be left open to imperialist propaganda, which seeks to blunt and distract the vigilance of the masses and spreads the slander that Communists do not oppose war and that they believe in the slogan 'the worse the better' because they wish to achieve Socialism by means of war. If we do not refute calumnies of this kind with clear pronouncements on the possibility of avoiding imperialist war and do not work continuously to organize the masses for the defence of peace, we risk losing the sympathy of the broad masses, whose highest aspiration is the achievement of peace.[1]

It is worth injecting the remark that the 'calumnies and slanders' referred to by Longo, to the effect that Communists believed in the slogan 'the worse the better' and that they expected to achieve Communism through war had, until 1956 at the earliest, been nothing but the bare truth.

But the real crux of his speech came in his reply to the Chinese view that it was impossible to achieve Socialism (pre-Communism) by peaceful means. The Chinese, he said, had asked to be shown one country where the transition from capitalism to Socialism was being achieved by peaceful means, advancing continuously by developing democracy without insurrections and civil war, and without fresh wars between states. 'We reply, tranquilly and firmly, that the Communist Party of Italy has for some time been following this path.' And it was then that he went on to explain, as Togliatti was to do in greater detail later on, why the Italian Party was devoting so much time and energy not to propagating Communist doctrine but to fighting for what he called 'structural reforms' – all reforms, anywhere, of whatever kind, which were calculated to bring the workers more political power and improved material standards.

Longo was not alone at the 1960 Conference. He went farther

than the other delegates and he committed himself to a far more detailed particularization of his Party's aims. But his general line was echoed by others. Even Thorez of France, for long the bitter enemy of the Italian leadership, pleaded for the abandonment of outdated conceptions, including the use of the hallowed phrase 'the Dictatorship of the Proletariat'. The Swedes and the Swiss did not like this phrase either: it had never occurred to the Russians even to question it, and they must have been a little shocked when Hagberg of Sweden observed: 'This is an unattractive phrase in Sweden. . . . It is incorrect to try to analyse the events of the day by recourse to the theories of yesterday. . . . There is no sense in going on repeating what Lenin said once without taking note of the changes since his day.' It was Hagberg, too, who struck most clearly and unequivocally the note of reformism which Longo had sounded. The Swedish Communist Party, he said in effect, had given up fighting the Swedish Social Democrats, and they had no intention of ever resuming the fight. The Social Democrats had been in power in Sweden for many years, and it was childish to pretend that they were anything but a typically working-class party. Communists would get nowhere by abusing them. Further, and on a long-term view, the Swedish Communists had no desire to annihilate the Social Democrats: rather, they were working for the day when the two parties would be fused into one.

It is important to realize that these remarks by Longo, Hagberg, and others were not made for propaganda purposes in order to lull the Social Democrats of Europe, to disarm them into cooperation so that they might be ensnared and then swallowed up. That is the traditional Leninist strategy, and it has been employed, all too often with success, on numerous occasions. If Longo and Hagberg had been speaking at a public meeting it would have been correct, imperative indeed, to suspect a trick and to view their words with the utmost scepticism. But here there was no trick: their audience consisted exclusively of Communists, the élite of the international Communist leadership at that, meeting in solemn conclave to thresh out a policy declaration to serve as a guide in years to come.

In an earlier chapter I touched on the manner in which the true Leninist regarded the reformist, the social democrat, as the most vicious heretic, and how he had fallen so much in love with a particular means to social revolution that in his eyes the means had become more important than the end. But now, in the Moscow Kremlin in November 1960, here were Longo of Italy, representing the largest Communist Party outside the bloc (apart from the very special Indonesian Party), Hagberg, and others too, all insisting that the end was more important than the means. It was a momentous reversal. It was motivated not only by fear of nuclear war, but more particularly by recognition of the vast social changes that had taken place in Europe and North America since Lenin's day. Only the European Communists committed themselves to this reversal, and for obvious reasons: for the comrades of Guatemala or Viet-Nam there was not much hope in reformism, in the amelioration of the life of the masses by swift economic progress: violence seemed more useful to them. But all the same, they were not howled down, they were not even challenged. And although their thinking was far ahead of the thinking of the Russians, nobody contradicted them, nobody but the Chinese. And what they said was very near to what Khrushchev in the Soviet Union, Gomulka in Poland, Kadar in Hungary, were beginning, without saying so, in practice to do.

The formal Chinese reply was not made until Togliatti had publicly propounded this line at the Italian Party Congress in December 1962. Then *People's Daily* said:

After reading Togliatti's general report and concluding speech at the tenth Congress of the Italian Communist Party . . . one cannot help feeling that he and certain Italian Party leaders are departing further and further from Marxist-Leninism. . . .

They cherish the greatest illusions about imperialism, they deny the fundamental antagonism between the two world systems of Socialism and capitalism and the fundamental antagonism between the oppressor and the oppressed nations, and in place of international class struggle and anti-imperialist struggle they advocate international class collaboration among countries with different social systems and the establishment of a 'new international order'.

In the last analysis, the stand taken by Togliatti and certain other Italian Party leaders boils down to this – *the people of the capitalist countries should not make revolutions, the oppressed nations should not*

*wage struggles to win liberation, and the people of the world should not
fight against imperialism.** In fact all this exactly suits the needs of the
imperialists and the reactionaries.

And again, speaking this time of peaceful co-existence:

The principle of peaceful co-existence can apply only to relations
between countries with different social systems, not to relations
between oppressed and oppressor nations, nor to relations between
oppressed and oppressor classes. For an oppressed nation or people
the question is one of waging a revolutionary struggle to overthrow
the rule of imperialism and the reactionaries: it is not, and cannot be,
a question of peaceful co-existence with imperialism and the reactionaries.

But Togliatti and those who attack China extend their idea of
'peaceful co-existence' to cover relations between the colonial and
semi-colonial people on the one hand and the imperialists and colonial-
ists on the other. They say 'the problem of starvation which still
afflicts a billion people' and 'the problem of developing the productive
forces and democracy in the undeveloped areas' 'must be solved
through negotiations, seeking reasonable solutions and avoiding
actions which might worsen the situation and cause irreparable
consequences.' They do not like sparks of revolution among the
oppressed nations and peoples. They say that a tiny spark may lead
to a world war.

And then, taking up one of Togliatti's more revolutionary
ideas:

Even more astonishing is the fact that Togliatti and certain other
people extend their idea of class collaboration in the international
arena to cover 'joint intervention' in the undeveloped areas. They
have said that 'States of diverse social structure' can, through mutual
cooperation, 'jointly intervene' to bring about progress in the undeveloped areas. To talk like this is obviously to spread illusions in the
interest of neo-colonialism.[2]

2

How are we to sort out this confusion? It is clear by now that
what confronts us is very far from being a straightforward
doctrinal dispute between the present leaders of the two most

* My italics.

powerful Communist states, a dispute between close allies, or brothers, which can be resolved by the exercise of a little tact, a small concession by either or both. What we are assisting at is much more than this: it is nothing less than a complex, perhaps cataclysmic, process of fission within the Communist movement as a whole.

It is a process, moreover, in which a great many Communist parties are actively involved. Passivity is at a discount. It is true that certain parties – for example the French – content themselves with the apparently simple, if agonizing, decision of choice between Moscow and Pekin; but choice itself is action, and Communists, accustomed for so long to absolute obedience, are not well trained in choosing. It is true that in some parties choice itself is evaded: they proclaim neutrality; but this very neutrality is itself as a rule a product of conflicting forces within the individual party – for example the British (Mr Gollan's whole-hearted acceptance of the Soviet line has been opposed by many of his colleagues). Other parties, on the other hand, most notably the Italian, not only show great activity in supporting their chosen champion but seek to push him (in this case Khrushchev) farther and faster than he wishes to go.

The conflict itself, seen in isolation, is the product of an amalgam of all sorts of motives and impulses, some of them having nothing intrinsically to do with Communism, which defy exact analysis and methodical tabulation. But the confusion in our own minds is surely, at least in part, a reflection of the confusion in the minds of the champions of the opposed causes.

Thus, there are genuine differences of doctrine between China and the Soviet Union – and these are the differences which have been most sharply emphasized in all public polemics. But what is doctrine? When held by a practical politician, a man of action, as distinct from a studious theorist, remote from the life of action, can such a thing be said to exist?

There are also differences arising directly from feelings of nationalism. Anybody who still believes that nationalism has been eradicated by Communism will believe anything. The Soviet Union survived the last war not because the people were fighting for Communism (which most of them detested anyway) but because they were fighting for their country. The Communists of Yugoslavia rebelled against Stalin not because they disagreed with Moscow doctrine but because they objected to Russian domination. Gomulka was able to put himself forward as the Communist leader of an anti-Communist people in 1956 because he was the only man in sight who could stand up against Moscow. Communist Poles still detest Communist Germans, and Communist Germans still despise Communist Slavs. The Hungarian uprising was directed against Russian domination as much as against the Hungarian Communist system. Communist Rumanians oppress their unfortunate Transylvanian minorities and quarrel with Communist Hungarians on classical irredentist lines. We can follow this process round the world and come back to the Soviet Union where Great Russians, as always, lord it over the minority peoples of the Soviet Union.

Why should Sino–Soviet relations be exempt from this rule? And here it is not only nationalism that is involved but also racialism: the Russians to the Chinese are clumsy, hectoring, pink-skinned Europeans: 'Baldy Khrushchev' is something not far removed from a 'foreign devil'. The Chinese, to the Russians – growing increasingly colour-conscious – are yellow.

Feelings of nationalism and racialism are augmented by great-power rivalry. And this rivalry itself exists on two separate levels. There is the rivalry which would exist between China and the Soviet Union as great powers, one Euro–Asian, one Asian, no matter what social systems they constructed for themselves. And there is the rivalry which springs from the fact that both are Communist powers, each determined to be seen as the true inheritors of Lenin's authority. And this last ambition is induced not only by the search for true doctrine but also by the pursuit of international influence and prestige.

Cutting right through this perfectly understandable rivalry, and complicating nationalistic feelings intolerably, is the tension set up by the hopeless contradiction implicit in the fact that one of the great rivals, China, quite desperately requires material assistance from the other.

Add to all this the differences produced by discrepant appreciations of the international situation in general, above all the strength and weakness of the 'imperialist camp', and of the dangers and consequences of nuclear war in particular. These appreciations have in themselves nothing to do with ideology – and yet they are inextricably entangled with ideology. Both sides are doing their best to arrive at an objective assessment; but in fact each assessment is coloured by divergent doctrine and, when made, modifies doctrine.

The argument is thus circular. For us it is complicated still further by the impossibility of knowing to what extent each side is consciously, to what extent unconsciously, distorting its objective appreciations and its doctrinal assertions in order on the one hand to deceive itself and on the other to make propaganda – propaganda directed not only at the outside world but also within the 'Socialist camp' and among fraternal parties outside the camp.

Indeed, the only way to sort things out is to turn for a moment from the terms of the formal debate and to glance at what Moscow and Pekin are in fact doing and preaching – preaching because what they say in their sermons, as distinct from their disputations, is the word – to be translated by comrades all over the world into deeds.

Khrushchev, in the light of the nuclear threat, is not only determined to avoid a major war but is also urging other Communist lands to avoid minor wars which might lead to a major one. He has modified Lenin's doctrine in order to justify this policy. The Chinese, although they taunt Khrushchev with cowardice and insist that Communism could survive a nuclear war and should be ready to face one, show no signs of inviting Armageddon. They have not attacked Formosa, Hong Kong, or Portuguese Macao, as Khrushchev himself has pointed out. In the Indian affair they calculated, correctly, that their aggression would not invite retaliation from the West. They have been circumspect in south-east Asia.

Again, Khrushchev makes a great show of supporting neutralist governments and co-existing with 'imperialist' ones. The Chinese attack him for this, but they themselves show no scruples in giving aid where they can to underdeveloped countries – for example in Africa – where it appears to suit their purpose. They seek to trade extensively with 'the enemy', and while attacking the Russians for giving aid to India they themselves blandly negotiate a frontier agreement with Pakistan.

As for assisting revolutionary struggles, they have certainly done this in Laos and Viet-Nam, though with considerable discretion; but, considering the trained man-power at their disposal, they have been positively backward in active assistance. Moreover, as Khrushchev himself pointed out at the Moscow Conference in one of his interventions, Pekin had done great harm to the Communist movement in Indonesia by championing the *comprador* exploiters, simply because they were Chinese.

When it comes to disarmament and co-existence, Khrushchev has made universal disarmament into one of the main planks of his platform, and the Chinese object to this. But in fact the Soviet Union has not disarmed, and shows no signs of doing so, while his talk about co-existence has not prevented him from taking what action he conveniently could take to weaken the West and shatter its unity and work against its influence in the world at large.

Indeed, in practice there appears to be only one point on which Chinese and Soviet policy is actively opposed – the matter of coming to terms with America. Even here the difference is less than appears at first sight. From a strictly ideological point of view there is no difference between Khrushchev's attitude to the U.S.A. and Mao's attitude towards Pakistan. Khrushchev finds it expedient to be on good terms with America and with India, but on bad terms with the German Federal Republic. Mao finds it expedient to be on good terms with Pakistan and Burma, to trade with Canada and Australia, but to be on bad terms with America and India. Ideology does not come into it.

Indeed, the more we look at the problem the more, in a certain important sense, the ideological quarrel seems to boil down to little more than a smoke-screen. We have dwelt on it at length in this narrative, because both the Russians and the Chinese insist that we should do so. And there are, quite clearly, ideological differences. But these on examination turn out to be differences of emphasis rather than differences of principle, and they are certainly not yet, at any rate as far as professions of belief go, enough in themselves to account for the bitterness of the conflict.

Perhaps smoke-screen is the wrong image. Perhaps, rather, we should say that in this great conflict ideology is not the end but the means, that ideology is being used by both sides as a weapon in the struggle.

But what struggle? It can only be the struggle between two neighbouring powers for self-assertion, if not for dominion.

We cannot at this stage even begin to prophesy what the future holds. There are too many imponderables, too many unknowns in even the simplest equation – Russia versus China in, as it were, a vacuum. But Russia and China are far from existing in a vacuum, and any equation that had a remote bearing on reality would have to allow for the present intentions and the future behaviour not merely of continents and blocs but of countless individual countries. To move only a few miles from Vladivostok: how will Japan fit into any developing pattern? Nearer home still: we have a shrewd idea of how the Soviet Union will develop; but who can tell how Communist China will develop?

But although we may have a shrewd idea of how the Soviet Union will develop, that is as a great nationalist power moving farther from revolutionary preoccupations, we do not know what she is at this moment of time. That is to say, we do not know, and there is no means of knowing for certain, to what extent the ideology now being used by Khrushchev as a weapon is preached by him because it is expedient to preach it, and to what extent he himself is its slave. If Communist China did not exist would Khrushchev be talking so much about ideological warfare, about bloc antagonisms, about the irresistible advance of Communism? How much of this talk derives from conviction? How much from the need, as the head of a great power, to prevent his extra-territorial influence as leader of the world Communist movement, a great disruptive movement, from being wrested from him by the head of a neighbouring great power? It is my belief that Khrushchev, a born pragmatist viewing the world, inevitably, through Marxist spectacles, revived and built up the discredited Communist Party in the Soviet Union, seen as a most powerful administrative machine, by invoking the authority of Lenin in order to win power for himself. Having achieved power, he now has to go on invoking Lenin or else see the leadership of the Communist movement fall into Chinese hands. But this cannot be proved.

So we are left with the obvious. The Sino–Soviet conflict exists and will continue. The Soviet Union possesses nuclear arms; China does not. China has asked Russia for these arms, and Russia has refused to supply them. Why? Because Khrushchev fears that China may use them recklessly and plunge the world into a war of annihilation? Or because, in traditional Russian style, he prefers not to have a strong China up against his own frontier? No doubt for both reasons. And quite apart from these fears, it could hardly be expected that Khrushchev, or any other Soviet leader, would view with anything but dismay the establishment of a strong centralized power, equipped with nuclear arms, which regarded the whole of Asia as its own sphere of influence.

It is not at all necessary at this stage to speculate about the possibility of armed conflict between China and the Soviet Union. Or, rather, it is enough to say that in the nuclear age the whole range of traditional thinking about war and peace has become irrelevant and meaningless, no matter how desperately the governments of the world and their military advisers may cling – as they do, inevitably, cling – to antiquated concepts. Twenty years ago it would have been permissible to predict that two powers finding themselves in the position in which China and the Soviet Union find themselves today would, sooner or later, start shooting. China has already hinted to the Soviet Union that the day may conceivably come when, if Moscow does not behave itself, she will lay claim to various Soviet territories in the extreme south-east of the Union which were obtained for Russia by the Tsarist regime in disreputable circumstances. It is improbable, to say the least, that the two powers would ever embark on a nuclear war to settle this matter. But it is not in the least improbable that limited border conflicts might arise, involving parts of these territories, or the Mongolias, which could lead to a state of undeclared war. Nor is it inconceivable that China could one day exert a blackmailing pressure on the Soviet Union to force her to open up her vast, unpopulated Siberian lands to Chinese settlers – or that the Russians might reach agreement with Tokyo designed, precisely, to forestall such action. Detailed speculation, as I have said, is useless. But it should be borne constantly in mind that there is nothing immutable about the present boundaries and power relations at present defining the limits of Soviet, Chinese, Japanese, and Indian activity. This would be true no matter what sort of political regime existed in those countries.

3

But in fact both China and the Soviet Union have Communist regimes. This fact obviously makes for a strong community of interest; but it is a community of interest which has been quite recklessly, one might almost say hysterically, exaggerated. There have been other communities of interest. Most of the wars of which we in the West are historically conscious have been fought between powers fervently professing Christianity. Catholic has fought against Catholic, Protestant against Protestant. Christians have not hesitated to ally themselves with Muslims against fellow-Christians. Catholics have allied themselves with heretics against fellow-Catholics. That Communists are prepared if necessary to fight against Communists – and to seek capitalist aid in their struggle – we know from the Yugoslav experience. In fact we ought to know this, Yugoslavia or no Yugoslavia, just as Professor Pavlov ought to have known that dogs salivate when they hear the dinner bell, without setting up cruel experiments to prove it. Gomulka even was prepared to fight Khrushchev.

What we took for a united front, a monolithic bloc of the faithful, was the Soviet Communist empire ruled by Stalin's police, backed by Stalin's army. In the early days of the Chinese revolution it was very much in the interests of both Stalin and Mao Tse-tung to pretend that China and the Soviet Union were united by unbreakable bonds – ideological bonds. From Stalin's point of view the keeping up of this pretence on the Chinese side meant that the Chinese would have to toe the line for the time being; *his* line. From the Chinese point of view this contrived bogey of Sino–Soviet unity was useful for frightening the rest of the world, above all America. But it takes two to make a scarecrow effective, and the crows have only themselves to blame if they take a ragged coat and a billy-cock hat on a pole for Farmer Giles with a gun. But it is outside the scope of this book to consider the nature of the madness which made the West believe either that the proud and mighty Chinese would submit indefinitely to dictation from the Russian barbarians (with Mao as a sort of Asian Ulbricht), or that Moscow and Pekin, just because both of them chose to recognize Lenin as their paraclete, would march forward in unison down the corridors of the years . . . To what? We are concerned, rather, with Russian and China as powers, and with Russia and China as Communist conspirators.

We have seen how far the Soviet Union has moved in practice from Leninist ideals; and we have seen how far certain of the European Communist Parties are moving away from those ideals in theory – above all the Italian Party, the white hope of the movement. But Europe is not all, and the sophistications of Messrs Togliatti and Hagberg and even M. Thorez are of very little interest to their fraternal comrades in Nicaragua, in Guinea, in Indonesia, in Egypt (those whom Nasser has not shot). They will be of very little interest to the Communist Parties, either small and proscribed, or not yet born, which will sooner or later make themselves felt in all the newly independent or not yet independent realms of Africa. In Western Europe, indeed, the Communist Parties, unless seen as agents of Russian power, are already anachronistic: the vast majority of French and Italian Communist voters, upon whom Messrs Togliatti and Thorez depend for the effects, are not Communists at all in the Leninist sense: they are left-wing protestants. There was indeed a day when they could have been useful as fifth columnists for an expanding Russian empire; but the bomb has put an end to that sort of light-hearted empire-building. In Britain the anachronistic nature of the Communist Party has been recognized by what the Russians (almost alone in our age outside a handful of British and European stately homes) like to call the working class. It has only 30,000 members, and that in a country where, in spite of reassuring noises to the contrary, the condition of millions is still a national disgrace. In the U.S.A. with its Poor Whites, poorer Blacks, and a habit of mind which sees nothing desperately wrong in a chronic burden of five million unemployed and which thinks that people should dutifully die for Old Glory or end up in the bankruptcy courts rather than get their hospitals free, the Communist Party is a non-starter.

In Britain, in Western Europe, only a lunatic fringe of Communists have ever really wanted to be taken over by Moscow. And even with them, I imagine, this desire is only an idiosyncratic form of the death-wish, so wide-spread today, which manifests itself elsewhere in the form of a quest for leadership and strong governments. Far more would like Britain, France, Italy, to follow the Soviet example, or what they imagine, or imagined, the Soviet example to be. Disgruntled scientists want big labs, paid for by the State. Best-selling novelists (not necessarily Communists either) think it would be nice to measure their sales in millions rather than in tens of thousands and be given government receptions in their honour into the bargain. Square pegs in round holes are irresistibly attracted to the squarest square of all (how they would rattle in it!). The conspiratorially-minded find a conspiracy on a scale beyond their silliest imaginings. The rancorous slip into an existence that might have been ordered for them; they can hate everybody and get a pat on the back for their spleen. All those weighed down by a sense of inferiority and frustration can bloom in a secret society which knows how to capitalize those qualities and inflate them with a sense of secret power. Others, cross and impatient idealists, find themselves harnessed to a powerful machine which, like Holy Church, assures them that perfect obedience will convey them to the kingdom of heaven without any need for self-propulsion on their part.

Russia for a long time was their Rome. But will Russia do much longer? Those British and European Communists who have achieved a vested interest in their ridiculous secret society, as well as those who are *actively* working for radical reform in their own countries, will doubtless continue to look to Moscow, if only because the Soviet Union is large and powerful and knows a trick or two. But those who are not happy unless they can feel that they are on the inside track of history? And those who really believe that what Communism is for is to achieve (through the dictatorship of the proletariat, of course) a terrestrial paradise of equity and equality? What has Russia now to offer them? Let it not be thought that I am scorning, as Mao would put it, the Russian people or the Soviet achievement. On the contrary, from the Russian people we have much to learn about life, and from the Soviet system, though with very great reservations, a great deal about social organization. But the lessons that the Russians and the Soviet Union have to offer the world have nothing to do with Communism, but, rather, with anti-Communism. Communists outside the Soviet Union have nothing to learn (the lessons are for the rest of us) from their great brother beyond a few organizational, disciplinary, and conspiratorial tricks. But they still have something to learn from China. Khrushchev must know this very well. Obviously he will not surrender the advantage afforded by the leadership of a worldwide subversive movement without a struggle. Yet any active effort to retain it must sooner or later force him into courses in Latin America, in Africa, in Asia which will not only be dangerous in themselves but which will also alienate his European brothers.

China is not thus inhibited. She is still, after fifteen years of stable, if cruel, central government, an international pariah with much less to lose than the Soviet Union. For a long time the Russians must have blessed America for doing their work for them by so determinedly excluding the Chinese from the United Nations; but they must sometimes wonder now whether this was quite such a good idea as it looked earlier on. The powerful and unscrupulous government of a land of 650 million operating on its own, completely untrammelled by any international obligations of any kind, however tenuous, is a disconcerting element in itself. When that government makes a determined bid for the moral leadership of the existing Communist Parties of the backward countries and offers a focus for embryo parties in many lands where politics has so far not moved out of the tribal stage, it becomes formidable indeed. Mao Tse-tung almost certainly believes that the future for India, for Africa, belongs to Communism. This is the very spectre he invokes to frighten not us (who are not worth frightening) but Russia. What does Khrushchev believe? And what happens when Khrushchev goes?

It should be clear by now that nothing short of the removal of Khrushchev, by death, retirement, or deposition, can heal the breach. It should also be clear that, even if Khrushchev went and the Chinese decided to take the line that with his departure there was no obstacle to complete reconciliation and to make appeasing gestures to his successor, the basic cause of the conflict would remain. Between the Soviet Union and China there is a straightforward conflict of power and prestige as between two great powers bordering each other and growing mightily: the Soviet Union with 220 million increasing at the rate of 3 million a year and striving desperately to develop and fill up the great empty spaces of Siberia; China with between 600 and 700 million, increasing at the rate of 20 million a year, and with very much less space. The ideological differences are bound up with these basic facts, and, even if Moscow and Pekin could reach apparent ideological compromise, the movement would still be split. The sophisticated Parties of Western Europe are moving ever farther not only from the Chinese position but also from the position set out in the Moscow Declaration of 1957. Listen again to Signor Longo, speaking at Moscow in November 1960:[3]

... we must use these democratic institutions as tools for furthering the real power and effective influence of the working masses, we must integrate these institutions with new forms of democracy, including that of direct democracy. ... Particular importance is vested in ... the struggle for what we call structural reform ... measures that tend to place effective restrictions on the power of the great monopolies over the nation's entire life, to nationalize certain industries, to establish forms of democratic control over certain sectors of the national economy, to bring about far-reaching agrarian reforms, and so on. These aims ... were once generally defined in the Communist movement as aims of a transitional character. Lenin considered it allowable and necessary for the Communist Party, under certain circumstances, and particularly in periods of revolutionary crisis, to adopt such aims as these. ... *We believe that in the present phase of history, and particularly in certain countries, such as Italy, the planning of the struggle for such goals as these is an important and permanent task of a Communist Party. ...*

* My italics.

Different roads ... If one thing is certain, it is that the world Communist movement, as a monolithic phenomenon controlled from a single centre, whether Moscow or Pekin, is finished. This is not to say that Communist Parties in all lands, including Britain, will cease to exist as highly disruptive forces, operating either in the interests of the Soviet Union (or China) as a power, or in order, through fissile action, to seize power for themselves. It is simply to say that there can no longer be any question of the existence of a single master plan. In future, each Communist Party, each Communist-controlled country must be studied individually and treated individually.

There remains China, a threat to us all, including the Soviet Union. It may be that Communist China will collapse under her own weight. But at present there are no signs of this happening. She has come through her worst food crisis, and today the rigid commune doctrine of 1958 is ameliorated by the existence of millions of tolerated private plots, tended by individuals toiling as individuals. She appears to have succeeded in adapting her industry to the situation created by the effective withdrawal of Soviet aid. Moscow can still blackmail her by threatening to cut off oil supplies, can still withhold atomic weapons and modern arms of every kind. But it seems likely that China will survive, an independent power of colossal size, proclaiming a revolutionary creed, at least for decades to come, and creating problems on a scale to match her size and her contempt of the West, including Russia.

A NOTE ON SOURCES

I HAVE kept the notes to the minimum. Sources for statements and quotations which are in the field of common knowledge have not been cited. For the greater part of the book the main sources are the Soviet and Chinese press and an assortment of Communist Party policy documents. For a detailed analysis of the dispute between China and the Soviet Union up to 1961, the reader is referred to *The Sino–Soviet Conflict* by Donald S. Zagoria (Princeton University Press and Oxford University Press, 1962), which is elaborately documented. Many of the more important documents cited in the narrative are to be found in English translation in *The Sino–Soviet Dispute*, Documented and Analysed by G. F. Hudson, Richard Lowenthal, and Roderick MacFarquhar (published by the *China Quarterly*, London, 1962). The files of the *China Quarterly* itself provide a mine of information. Important Soviet and Chinese policy documents may as a rule be obtained in pamphlet form from Messrs Collett's Russian Bookshop, Museum Street, London WCI.

Chapters 10, 11, and 12, in which I summarize the proceedings of the Bucarest and Moscow Conferences, are based largely on the material which I used for articles on the state of Sino–Soviet relations in the *Observer* on 12 and 19 February 1961 and in the *Atlantic Monthly* for May 1961 and June 1963.

The authenticity of these accounts has already been amply confirmed by material on the Moscow Conference which the Italian, French, and Belgian Communist Parties have published from their own archives. Anyone who is interested in seeing the proceedings of the second half of 1960 in perspective is recommended to read in the *China Quarterly*, No. 11, 1962, a fascinating article by William E. Griffith entitled 'The November 1960 Moscow Meeting: a Preliminary Reconstruction'. This is itself fully documented. The main sources bearing closely on Chapters 10–12 of this book are: *Interventi della delegazione del P.C.I. alla Conferenza degli 81 partiti communisti* (Sezione centrale di stampa e propaganda della Direzione del P.C.I.: Rome, 15 January 1962); several articles in the newspaper of the

Belgian Communist Party, *Le Drapeau rouge*, during January, February, and March 1962; *Contribution de la délégation française à la conférence des partis communistes et ouvriers, Moscou, Novembre 1960* (Parti Communiste Français, Paris, November 1961); and *Problèmes du mouvement communiste international*, édité par le Comité Central du Parti Communiste Français (Paris, January 1963).

There are occasional references in the text, outside Chapters 10–12, to the material on the Bucarest and Moscow conferences, referred to above, which is referred to in the Notes which follow as the Bucarest Documents and the Moscow Documents.

Notes

Chapter 6

1. Moscow Documents.
2. *Ibid.*
3. *Ibid.*

Chapter 7

1. The Text of Moscow Declaration is contained in *The Sino–Soviet Dispute, cit. supra.*
2. *Red Flag*, Pekin, 3 March 1963.
3. To the Chungking conference of cadres, reported by the New China News Agency, 17 May 1957.
4. To the National People's Congress, reported by the New China News Agency, 1 July 1957.
5. See *Imperialism and All Reactionaries are Paper Tigers*, Foreign Languages Press, Pekin, 1958.

Chapter 8

1. To the 8th Party Congress, 5 May 1958, reported in *Pekin Review*, 14 June 1958.

Chapter 9

1. For the Marshal Peng story see 'The Dismissal of Marshal Peng Teh-huai' by David A. Charles in the *China Quarterly*, No. 8, 1961.
2. Moscow Documents.
3. At a reception given at the Indonesian Embassy, reported by the New China News Agency, 27 August 1959.

4. *Problems of Peace and Socialism*, November 1959.

5. Moscow Documents and *Drapeau rouge*, Brussels, 22 February 1962. See also *Interventi* (*cit. supra*) and *Contribution* (*cit. supra*) for the Italian and French C.P. versions.

6. An English translation is to be found in *The Sino–Soviet Dispute* (*cit. supra*).

7. Speech delivered in Moscow, 22 April 1960, *Pravda*, 23 April 1960.

8. Moscow Documents.

Chapters 10–12

These three chapters are based wholly on the Bucarest and Moscow Documents (see *A Note on Sources, supra*) and the 1960 Moscow Declaration, the English text of which is contained in *The Sino–Soviet Dispute* (*cit. supra*). Notes 1 and 2 in Chapter 12 refer to *Contribution de la délégation française* and *Le Drapeau rouge*, 22 February 1962 (*cit. supra*).

Chapter 14

1. *Interventi, cit. supra.*

2. *People's Daily*, 31 December 1962.

3. *Interventi.*

*Some other books published by
Penguins are described on
the following pages*

Voters, Parties, and Leaders

THE SOCIAL FABRIC OF BRITISH POLITICS

J. BLONDEL

A638

Are we witnessing the end of class-barriers in the political behaviour of the British voter? Does the businessman vote like the railwayman, the white-collar worker like the unskilled labourer?

Of course they do not. But how different are their voting habits? Trade Unions are Labour-inclined, but all trade unionists are not Labour men. Are these non-Labour trade unionists exceptional. And, at the other end of the scale, are Labour-inclined professional people, managers, and executives rare but interesting exceptions?

These are some of the questions which the newly appointed Professor of Government in the University of Essex attempts to answer in this original book. In examining the background, outlook, and interests of voters, party members, politicians, civil servants, and party leaders, and endeavouring to trace some of the subtle threads that tie certain individuals to certain organizations, he presents an anatomy of the political world. And he asks: 'What is the "Establishment" we talk of? Does it exist? And if so, does it rule?'

A History of British Trade Unionism

HENRY PELLING

A616

Today trade unionism plays a more important part in the nation's economy than ever before, and its problems of internal reform and its relations with the government and the public are constantly under discussion. But its present structure can only be understood in relation to its long history. And, indeed, its history in Britain is also the first chapter in the history of trade unionism all over the world.

In this, the first comprehensive book on the subject for thirty-five years, Henry Pelling, a Fellow of the Queen's College, Oxford, and author of *The Origins of the Labour Party*, leads the reader through a vivid story of struggle and development covering more than four centuries: from the medieval guilds and early craftsmen's and labourers' associations to the dramatic growth of trade unionism in Britain in the nineteenth and twentieth centuries. Most important, he traces the course of two significant issues: first, the shift in power from the craft unions to the amalgamated unions, and finally in our time to the giant general unions. And, secondly, the changing relationships of the labour and political functions of the unions from the early nineteenth century through the Labour Representation Committee to the block vote and the 1959 Labour Party Conference.

Trade Unions are an essential party of our society and we must understand them if we are to understand Britain today.

The Theory and Practice of Communism

R. N. CAREW HUNT

A578

'This is the best short account of Marxism and its Russian consequences written from a highly critical standpoint that has come my way' – Edward Crankshaw in the *Observer*.

R. N. Carew Hunt has come to be recognized as one of the greatest Western authorities on communism. This concise and critical study of Marxism and its interpretation in practice has quickly gained the standing of a classic. The author clearly demonstrates that modern Marxism is a synthesis, in which the basic creed of Karl Marx and Engels has been tailored by Lenin and Stalin to fit the twentieth century. In its analysis of the relationship and the contrasts between Marx's predictions and the policies of the communist governments of today the book provides an excellent outline of the institutions and events which have helped to shape the map of the contemporary world – the Communist League, the First and Second Internationals, the Russian Revolution, and developments both inside and outside Russia between the time of Lenin and Khrushchev.

The author's view of communism is rigorously critical, but never unreasoning: he is concerned, first and foremost, to expound the most dynamic creed of the last hundred years.

'A good book for the non-Marxist and the Marxist' – Bertrand de Jouvenal in *Time and Tide*.

Unarmed Victory

BERTRAND RUSSELL

S220

We have recently witnessed an unarmed victory of historic significance. The outcome of the Cuban crisis and of the frontier dispute between China and India has proved that the greatest powers, even when they have consolidated a position of strength, may still fight shy of the irremediable lunacy of modern war. The Russians and the Chinese voluntarily accepted compromise without loss of face.

In addressing himself directly to Kennedy, Khrushchev, Nehru, and Chou En-Lai, Bertrand Russell valiantly interposed the small voice of reason during those frightening weeks when we awoke every morning to the prospect of universal annihilation. In substance his proposals – as any reader of this Penguin Special can see – were calculated to achieve exactly what took place. The Russians never challenged the American blockade of Cuba and the guns were rested on the Himalayas.

Would it be too sanguine to conclude that the voice of one of the greatest thinkers of our time was heeded in the chancelleries? At any rate one reads this account of what one man did when the world was swaying on the brink of nuclear war with admiration and gratitude.

Great Britain or Little England?

JOHN MANDER

S222

'Britain has lost an Empire and not yet found a role,' stated Dean Acheson. Was he right?

In this thoughtful and disquieting essay John Mander, whose Penguin Special, *Berlin: Hostage for the West*, was described by the *Guardian* as a 'brilliant book', argues that since the war Britain has never clearly decided whether to be America's chief ally in the cold war, a mediator between America and Russia, the doyen of an independent Commonwealth, or one more recruit for the European community. Hence so many of our difficulties – the Suez débâcle, impotence during the Cuban crisis, humiliation over the Common Market, hopeless confusion over nuclear armaments.

We face another world today, and John Mander powerfully urges that we should at once re-think our position in it. In the sanest sense his exercise in *real-politik* – terrifying in its precision – is a book about patriotism by a patriot. At a time when old loyalties are dissolving into new, his conclusions are likely to be violently discussed.

NOT FOR SALE IN THE U.S.A.

The Making of Modern Russia

LIONEL KOCHAN

A529

'This is a history of Russia from the earliest times up to the outbreak of the Second World War. However, in keeping with his choice of title, Mr Kochan has concentrated on the modern period, devoting about as many pages to the eighty years following the Emancipation of the Serfs in 1861 as to the preceding 800-odd years. ... The result is a straightforward account of a complicated story. A successful balance has been held between such conflicting themes as foreign policy ... foreign influences and native intellectual trends ... His book could be a valuable introduction to the general reader in search of guidance ... a commendable book' – *Sunday Times*

'He handles his material with skill and sympathy. I cannot think of a better short book for acquainting the general reader with the broad outlines of Russian history. I hope many will read it' – Edward Crankshaw in the *Observer*

'Gives proper weight to economic, geographical, and cultural, as well as political and military factors, and which, while giving long-term trends their place, manages very often to convey a sense of real events happening to real people' – Wright Miller in the *Guardian*

'It reads easily, it is the ideal book for the general reader' – *The Economist*